Using Twitter to Build Communities

Using Twitter to Build Communities

A Primer for Libraries, Archives, and Museums

Valerie Forrestal
Tinamarie Vella

ROWMAN & LITTLEFIELD
Lanham • Boulder • New York • London

Published by Rowman & Littlefield
An imprint of The Rowman & Littlefield Publishing Group, Inc.
4501 Forbes Boulevard, Suite 200, Lanham, Maryland 20706
www.rowman.com

6 Tinworth Street, London SE11 5AL

British Library Cataloguing in Publication Information Available

Library of Congress Cataloging-in-Publication Data Available

ISBN 978-1-5381-0604-4 (hardback : alk. paper) | ISBN 978-1-5381-0605-1 (pbk. : alk. paper) | ISBN 978-1-5381-0606-8 (ebook)

∞™ The paper used in this publication meets the minimum requirements of American National Standard for Information Sciences—Permanence of Paper for Printed Library Materials, ANSI/NISO Z39.48-1992.

Printed in the United States of America

For Lauryn Okaly—V. F.

Contents

Figures

Preface

Research shows that educational institutions are failing to make the best use of Twitter, focusing mostly on branding instead of engagement. This presents educational organizations like archives, libraries, and museums with a great opportunity to jump in and use their own social media presence to interact with their communities and build excitement around their collections, services, and programs. This book provides concrete ways for archives, libraries, and museums to go far beyond Twitter as a "broadcasting" tool and highlights innovative methods to use the service to spark communication and create ties within your institution's greater community.

Appropriate for the social media beginner as well as the experienced user, it covers topics like drafting a social media policy, setting up a new or rebranding an existing institutional Twitter account, finding and interacting with your followers, successfully using hashtags and media, scheduling and automating posts, sharing information across social media platforms, and using analytics software to make connections and measure impact.

In short, this book condenses years of research and expertise on using Twitter in an institutional setting into one handy reference for launching or reviving your organization's Twitter presence into an impactful medium in your community. Many of us working in educational institutions find ourselves stretched very thin, and while creating a Twitter account for your archive, library, or museum might seem easy enough, the simple and practical guidance in this book will help maximize the impact and outreach of your Twitter presence, so your social media efforts are not wasted "shouting into the void."

Acknowledgments

When my coauthor, Valerie Forrestal, approached me about the idea of writing about Twitter, I never thought that I would be embarking on this magical journey into book publishing. Val, thank you for choosing me to tackle this with you! It was a great opportunity and very fitting after all—we did meet on Twitter many moons ago (sometime in 2009 to be exact).

I also want to take the time to acknowledge those that helped make this book become a reality:

The countless people that I interviewed via e-mail and in person. Some are featured in this book and others helped shape ideas and thoughts—I thank you for your time and passion for this subject. This book is about making connections and building engagement in your communities. This book wouldn't have happened without your expertise and willingness to share your stories.

My friends and colleagues for their pep talks, words of encouragement and inspiration, and for being great souls; I'm lucky to have a supportive group of people that I can count on!

An extra special thank you to my wonderful family (near and far—hi, Mom, Dad, Denise, Liana, and Juliana—your names are in a book!) for always supporting and encouraging me. You are always proud of my endeavors in the world of librarianship (even though sometimes you have no idea what I'm talking about, I love you all!).

And to my husband, Santos—you no longer have to share me with book deadlines—*soy toda tuya hoy y siempre.*

—T. V.

1

Getting Started

Twitter is a tool that can be used to share news and information about your organization with the world. The world, however, is an awfully big place, and institutional Twitter accounts can consume vast amounts of staff time and energy only to become another of many voices shouting into the void, hoping to be heard by the people and groups who matter. In order to make this effort worthwhile, an organization must consider their communities, first and foremost, and take the time to build strong, meaningful networks within them. By looking at Twitter as a community-building tool, rather than simply a broadcasting channel, you increase your entire organization's value to its constituency, and you plant roots that make it easier to curate impactful, relevant, and engaging content.

DRAFTING A SOCIAL MEDIA POLICY

Before thinking about community building through Twitter, you should think about drafting a social media policy for your organization. In order to do this, you will need to have the key players in your organization involved. If your organization has a marketing department, you should consult with them about social media policies. If you do not have a marketing department or someone dedicated to handling your social media policies, this task should still involve input from others; do not draft the policies without consulting the team around you.

First, let's address the term "social media policy." A policy can also be described in different ways:

social media strategy, social media guidelines, or simply a social media guide. This book will refer to it as a social media policy. When you begin the process of drafting your own, please feel free to use the terminology that works best for your organization. This section provides guidance on handling the task of drafting one and why it is an essential piece of information for your organization.

All social media policies should provide a brief mission statement about the organization. A brainstorm activity with key players in your organization will make this task easier. As noted, if you have a marketing department or a person dedicated to handling social media platforms in your organization, they will definitely need to be a part of drafting this social media policy. Do not leave these people out of the equation. This statement should describe what your organization stands for. It describes the function and purpose of your organization. Successful statements are short, concise, and to the point. It is helpful to describe your organization in three adjectives. Think about the image that your organization wants to project to its community. A less-is-more approach works best for creating a statement of this kind for your organization. You should think about your mission and goals before you think about drafting your social media policy.

So, what is social media? In the strict Merriam-Webster dictionary sense, it is: "forms of electronic communication (such as websites for social networking and microblogging) through which users create online communities to share information,

Figure 1.1.   Creative Commons image of social networks. *Creative Commons*

ideas, personal messages, and other content (such as videos)."

In other words, social media is a catch-all definition for all platforms of electronic communication where social interaction occurs. This is a phrase that has become a part of our daily interactions. It is in our personal and professional lives. Twitter is one platform of social media that has become a part of everyday lives. Most organizations will use more than Twitter to interact with their community, but this book will focus on how to build your Twitter community.

Figure 1.1 shows various icons of popular social media platforms. The Pew Research Center conducts a social media update every year. Facebook remains the most popular, but LinkedIn, Instagram, Pinterest, and Twitter have steadily remained in the top five. The latest full update can be found online: www.pewinternet.org/2016/11/11/social-media -update-2016/.

Keeping up with trends will keep your policy relevant, but your organization does not have to adopt each new social media trend. A social media policy should serve the community, and it is impossible to have a one-size-fits-all policy. Each platform of communication involves different purposes. There are overarching policy statements to implement, but the ways of interacting and building communities may differ. Be prepared to modify. Many make the mistake of thinking that policies are not needed. It may seem like everyone knows how to post on social media, but not having a policy can lead to confusion, lack of vision, and possible legal implications. Taking the time to draft a policy will save you time and effort in the long run. The next four sections assess what you need to think about when drafting this policy. These sections aim to provide your organization with the strategic vision that is needed for its social media policy.

Defining Your Audience

This is where you establish your organization's vision. We discussed the importance of having a mission statement for your organization. The mission statement is key to understanding how to serve your community. Your community is your audience. These are the people that you are trying

Twitter

- Community focus: Students and faculty. Predominantly focused on undergraduate students. Campus and community partners.
- Goal: Expand dissemination of news and updates related to library services, events, collections, facilities, and campus involvement to encourage library "awareness" and usage. Remain active, professional, and friendly in responses to promote genuine and helpful library interaction experiences. Demonstrate the library's connection and support to the UCF campus and community at large.
- Content for posts: Announcements, events, services, new resources, campus highlights, and quirky/fun things related to libraries/reading/Dr. Pegasus/etc.

- Posting frequency: Daily total of 6 posts; 3 shares/retweets and 3 posts related to library and/or the campus and community.
- Ongoing series: Faculty/staff highlights/publications, 21st Century Library Project progress, What's Coming to the CFE Arena (i.e., post about a book related to the coming speaker), upcoming workshops, librarian quotes
- Platform manager: Cindy Dancel

Figure 1.2. Excerpts of UCF's social media guidelines. *University of Central Florida Libraries*

to reach with social media platforms, such as Twitter. They are your followers, fans, likes, whatever the platform may call them, and these are people that you are serving. If you are not serving them properly, community building does not happen. Your audience directly influences your social media policy. Make sure that you serve their needs. Do not create a bunch of different social media accounts for the sake of having them. Look at what your community needs. Where do they look for information? Ask them what type of platforms they would like for your organization to use. If your social media policy and its platforms are not working, you need to revisit and adapt the policy. The policy should never be so rigid that it fails to connect to your community.

For example, in an academic library setting, your social media platforms may reach different communities who may be in different stages of their academic careers (faculty, staff, undergraduate students, graduate students, alumni); the policy should not be so narrow in scope that it fails to embrace change. Depending on your institution, your target

audience may differ, and it helps to rethink your policy based on platform. Cynthia Dancel, senior art specialist at University of Central Florida (UCF) Libraries (@ucflibrary), explained the process of how her organization uses platform guidelines in their social media policy. Platform guidelines are a great way to showcase and ensure that each platform has a defined space for you to modify and revise as needed. If your policy needs to be reworked, you can just rework your Twitter strategy. You can adapt it to meet those needs without having to rewrite the entire policy. This approach works to ensure that your policy does not fall into the trap of trying to be a one-size-fits-all or one that does not engage communities in different ways for different platforms. Each platform will operate differently, and having your policy highlight that will ensure that it is an effective social media policy.

The University of Central Florida Libraries also shows an emphasis on community focus and the goal of the particular platform. This is essential. Each platform will lend itself to a particular community. If you attempt to reach your community on the same platforms with the same goals, you are not doing your social media policy any justice. Take the time to sit down and assess your community focus and what you are trying to accomplish through social media. Once you define the community focus and the purpose for each social media platform, the policy begins to write itself.

Another example would be to look at the National Archives and Records Administration (NARA) for guidance. In your respective fields, there are organizations and associations that you can count on for guidance on best practices. The NARA has a robust site on how they plan to strategize their social media for the next three years (2017–2020). This type of information is readily available for free, and you can download and incorporate their strategies into your own organization as you create your own strategies. It is worth noting that the four goals of the NARA (2016) are much in line with the goals of this book:

1. tell great stories
2. deepen engagement
3. grow our audience
4. cultivate a community of practice

This book serves as a primer to guide archives, libraries, museums, and other nonprofit organizations in their social media practices. This book will focus on Twitter in particular and how to effectively utilize the best practices and tools in the world today.

Deciding on the Tone and Scope

When developing your social media policy, deciding your tone and scope is essentially equivalent to finding your voice. The way that you communicate and reach those in your community comes across in your tone and scope. Take into account which platforms your organization will decide to use; that decision shapes your tone and scope.

For example, if you are in a public library setting, and you allow your branch libraries to have their own social media accounts, you will note that the tone should be respectful and cordial. The tone creates the mood for your social media platforms. The

tone should sync nicely with your mission statement. This is why it is important to create a mission statement before you even address social media policies. Most will find that the best tones for social media platforms in general are conversational and ask questions and encourage discussion. When your tone is too rigid and formal, it seems standoffish and it will appear as though your organization does not want to engage with the community.

Buffer explains the difference between tone and voice really well and will help clarify any misunderstandings:

> The definitions that make the most sense to me are the ones that note a difference between voice and tone. Gather Content breaks down the difference in this way:
>
> Voice: Your brand personality described in an adjective. For instance, brands can be lively, positive, cynical, or professional.
>
> Tone: A subset of your brand's voice. Tone adds specific flavor to your voice based on factors like audience, situation, and channel.
>
> Essentially, there is one voice for your brand and many tones that refine that voice.
>
> Voice is a mission statement. Tone is the application of that mission. (Lee 2016)

Meanwhile, the scope is more of the parameters. It explains what content is relevant for particular platforms. For your different social media platforms, you may decide to showcase different types of content. There are various types of content to display, and based on which platform you choose, there may be parameters built into the platform. For example, Twitter has a 280-character limit for each post. This means that you need to be concise with your content. Looking at each platform and deciding the scope will reduce the need for redundancy among your social media platforms. You make the decision if you want to post different content on different platforms. The most effective strategy is usually that a good combination of original content on each platform works best. This is why the social media policy is so vital; it will help clarify your organization's vision.

The tone and scope needs to be addressed for each platform as this is the most effective way to draft a policy for your organization. Many organizations rely on style guides and communication policies in addition to social media policies in order to be successful in their social media strategic efforts. The more that you structure and detail the policy, the better it serves your community. This will become evident as you communicate with your community. If you attempt to start a social media effort without thinking about how you will sound or how you will be perceived by your community, you are on the way to having a failed social media effort.

Creating a "Brand"

With all that has been addressed so far, it should not surprise you that this is all about your brand. You may think you do not have one, but as Buffer perfectly sums it up, you most definitely need to think that you do: "You're right in assuming that brands refer to big and small companies who sell products and services. I'd also like to open up the definition to individuals as well. Coca-Cola has a brand. Pat's Corner Store has a brand. You have a brand. Basically, everyone on social media has a brand, whether they know it or not." (Lee 2016).

Your organization should be mindful of the image that it projects through social media. As stated before, your consultations with key players in your organization to receive approval of logos, banners, and/or images to use on your social media platforms should happen early on and before you begin your social media efforts. Make sure that these images are original and copyrighted for use in your organization.

Branding efforts are vital to success in any venture that your organization will undertake, but, when it comes to social media, marketing your organization equals success. In an e-mail interview, Maria Chiochios, who worked as management fellow at San Mateo County Libraries (SMCL) (@smclibraries), explained how their library system updated their brand and established a new brand style guide for their organization to use. This guide detailed everything from their new logo to color usage and how it would impact the brand of this particular organization. It may not seem significant, but creating and keeping with your brand makes a huge difference for your organization's image in the community.

There are a few key elements to keep in mind for branding your organization. First, choose a logo that defines your organization. This is your organization's headshot. Make it count. Don't skimp or slack on the design of the logo, and make sure it speaks to your community. Logos can make or break an organization. Second, color and font usage need to be consistent. On Twitter, there are default colors

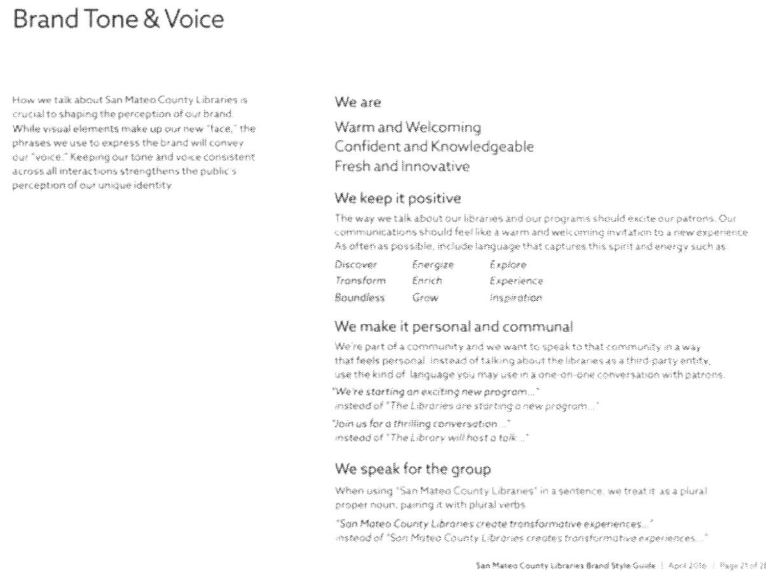
Brand Tone & Voice

How we talk about San Mateo County Libraries is crucial to shaping the perception of our brand. While visual elements make up our new "face," the phrases we use to express the brand will convey our "voice." Keeping our tone and voice consistent across all interactions strengthens the public's perception of our unique identity.

We are

Warm and Welcoming
Confident and Knowledgeable
Fresh and Innovative

We keep it positive

The way we talk about our libraries and our programs should excite our patrons. Our communications should feel like a warm and welcoming invitation to a new experience. As often as possible, include language that captures this spirit and energy such as:

Discover *Energize* *Explore*
Transform *Enrich* *Experience*
Boundless *Grow* *Inspiration*

We make it personal and communal

We're part of a community and we want to speak to that community in a way that feels personal. Instead of talking about the libraries as a third-party entity, use the kind of language you may use in a one-on-one conversation with patrons.

"We're starting an exciting new program..."
instead of "The Libraries are starting a new program..."

"Join us for a thrilling conversation..."
instead of "The Library will host a talk..."

We speak for the group

When using "San Mateo County Libraries" in a sentence, we treat it as a plural proper noun, pairing it with plural verbs.

"San Mateo County Libraries create transformative experiences..."
instead of "San Mateo County Libraries creates transformative experiences..."

San Mateo County Libraries Brand Style Guide | April 2016 | Page 21 of 28

Figure 1.3. Brand style guide from San Mateo County Libraries. ***San Mateo County Libraries***

and fonts, but this is important if you are creating promotional information and using it on Twitter. A general rule would be to think about the effect of certain fonts and colors and how your brand can be perceived. Be mindful of the color that your organization will use and how it can impact how your community interacts with you. Choose fonts and colors that are perceived as clear, focused, engaging, and inviting. Avoid colors and fonts that are confusing, harsh, and unapproachable. Taking note from *Entrepreneur*, and looking into the psychology of color and what it means to your community: "When it comes to picking the 'right' color, research has found that predicting consumer reaction to color appropriateness in relation to the product is far more important than the individual color itself. So, if Harley owners buy the product in order to feel rugged, you could assume that the pink + glitter edition wouldn't sell all that well" (Ciotti 2016).

Your brand trickles down into every facet of your organization, and particularly in social media, this may be the first time your community interacts with your organization. These social media policies can easily be adapted for your communications policies, in terms of how you communicate with your community. Social media is an integral part of your branding, and it should be given proper attention from your organization's key players. Having this conversation before you tackle any policies will make the process go more smoothly and more effectively. You will be thankful for having the hard conversations, rather than having to decide quickly if it will be approved or accepted for your policy.

To conclude with brand, tone, and scope, here are valuable tips from *Marketing Land*: "A social media voice can be hip, communal, playful, educational, sophisticated, fun, irreverent, inspirational, helpful or a million other adjectives. So how do you find your brand's voice? Explore the three Cs: culture, community and conversation" (Seiter 2012).

The three Cs—culture, community, and conversation—are what you also should be considering for your engagement strategy. The culture surrounding your organization is what makes your organization unique and special. This brings us to community and the people who you are trying to reach; this is your opportunity to listen and learn from them

to see what they want. And lastly, conversation is what culture and community will bring you; it is the style of natural, comfortable conversation occurring in a relaxed and not forced setting. Use the three Cs whenever you are unsure of your engagement strategy, as you are creating your strategy and implementing your policies. It will be your internal guide to craft your strategy or re-create as necessary.

Setting Rules for Language and Media Content

The rules for language and media content need to be in place to guide and regulate what will be allowed and tolerated on *all* social media platforms. Having these rules addressed upfront will ensure that there is no confusion between platforms.

When dealing with media content, there is a rule of 5:3:2. This was introduced by T. A. McCann at gist.com. This rule basically states that for every ten tweets or posts that are made on your organization's social media accounts, five of them should be from other organizations, curated by your organization, that are relevant to your community; three of them should be from your organization, relevant to your community; and two of them should be personal, showing a human side to your organization (Heinz 2011). This is a good rule of thumb regarding media content; it helps guide your platforms and allows room for administrators of these accounts to have the freedom to post what they feel works best.

With language, best to err on the side of caution, and be stricter about setting rules. Setting language rules can be as simple as not tolerating vulgar or inappropriate language. The same would apply to media content. When setting rules, it needs to be explicitly stated that your organization does not condone or tolerate vulgar, inappropriate language and content. But language can also be suggestive; as with tone and scope, you provide guidelines that lend to your mission and goals. San Mateo County Libraries do a great job of highlighting how to handle language, tone, and voice in their brand style guide. This excerpt provides great context for those interested in drafting this in their social media policies.

Your social media policy can be as detailed as your organization may need it to be. Follow a step-by-step process of addressing and assessing the four main components:

1. defining your audience
2. deciding on tone and scope
3. creating a "brand"
4. setting rules for language and media content

These components will allow you to draft a social media policy that works best for your organization and the community that you serve. After drafting the social media policy, you have now addressed why your organization wants to use social media and what the purpose is. You can now focus on your organization's mission and vision and start to build your community by utilizing the full potential of your social media engagement.

The key ingredients for a successful social media policy are that the policies should be platform based, not one-size-fits-all, and they should work for your community and be adaptive and engaging for your staff and community alike.

Gathering research on social media policies and guides on how to get started are part of the journey. A dated source with some advice that still remains true is from *College and Research Libraries News* (*CRLN*): "Just like any new library resource or initiative it is necessary to promote it. 'Build it and they will come' is not a viable strategy. 'Market it and they may take a look' is much more realistic" (Burkhardt 2010).

This continues to be solid advice when dealing with social media strategies. You cannot just expect your Twitter presence to work for itself; you have to put in the proper effort and do the research before starting to tweet. If you just start your presence without a strategy, you are setting it up to fail.

GETTING STARTED ON TWITTER

Choosing Account Administrators

If your institution has a marketing or outreach department or position, or even better, a "social media person," then deciding who should be in charge of your Twitter presence is fairly simple. However, in a tight budget climate for the arts and humani-

ties, this is often not the case for archives, libraries, and museums. Even when a marketing team or person is available, they may not be as familiar with specific social networks as they are with more traditional outreach methods. If your organization does decide to use Twitter for outreach and communication, and there is not an obvious person or team to administer the account, one or more staff members will need to be selected to post regular updates, monitor for mentions and respond when need be, and keep track of usage statistics. When selecting staff members to administer your institution's Twitter account, here are some factors to keep in mind:

1. *Enthusiasm and commitment:* Using Twitter successfully requires a time and energy commitment that people often underestimate. Finding people who are enthusiastic about connecting with their community through social media is important for making sure they can keep the commitment for more than just the short term. Keeping your Twitter account active and relevant can also require some amount of work off the clock. Administrators will generally have to monitor the account (usually just by keeping an eye out for notifications) on nights and weekends in case something time-sensitive comes through. They also have to keep abreast of trending news and events in order to keep the account topical, which can mean watching the nightly news or listening to relevant radio or podcasts during off-work hours.
2. *Familiarity with the medium:* Any online community (or any community, really) has patterns of behavior that are generally accepted and expected when interacting within the community. This includes not only technical issues like using system features but also conversational tone, language and grammar usage, linking and attribution, and use of images, audio, and video. It is best to have at least one account administrator who has used Twitter for a substantial period of time and who understands the "rules of the road" and can act as an advisor and sometimes editor for less experienced users.
3. *Familiarity with the web and digital media in general:* Twitter is not an island unto itself. It is

often a method of connecting your community to other parts of the Internet and other kinds of digital media. You might be linking to your website, your other social media accounts, or articles or videos in various formats on various platforms. It helps to have a firm grasp on how people generally navigate the Internet so you can know when and what kind of media best convey or enhance your message. It's also helpful to understand the technological demographics of your own community. Do most of them have smartphones and/or tablets? Are they tech-savvy in general? You don't want to frustrate them with media or links that are hard to open or difficult to navigate on a mobile device or complicated for them to interact with.

4. *Trustworthiness:* Obviously allowing a staff member to post content in your institution's name can be a bit of a risk. There are countless stories of employees "going rogue" and tweeting inappropriate things or accidentally tweeting personal content from an institutional account instead of their own. The nature of Twitter, being a fast-moving, real-time medium, makes it difficult for one person to always oversee all tweets before they are sent out, so account administrators should be staff members who have been with the institution long enough to have a history of reliability or should be individuals who successfully held a similar role at another organization. All account administrators should be well-trained in regard to the institution's social media policy and should have a contact they can go to with questions and concerns. There should also be a main account administrator who monitors the account and keeps an eye out for potential issues. Whenever an employee steps down as an account administrator, for whatever reason (even if on good terms), the account password should be changed.

5. *Good networking skills:* As mentioned above, Twitter works best when used as a network rather than a broadcasting tool. Your account administrators should have an affinity for, or at least be open to, seeking out connections wherever possible. This can mean reaching out to other departments within your institution or other like-minded organizations or individuals. Building a strong network means you can cross-promote your collections and events with other groups and also means being able to target the best channels for promoting specific content or creating lively discourse around desired topics. If there is a person in your organization who regularly deals with other communication outlets, either in your institution or in the local community, that person should definitely be involved in your Twitter campaigns, since they will have the contacts to promote your tweets in the larger circles that your organization exists within.

6. *Through understanding of purpose:* Finally, to keep your institution's Twitter presence interesting and engaging, account administrators should post diverse content from a variety of sources, but underneath it all there needs to be a common thread, or underlying purpose. This purpose should be spelled out in your social media policy and should stem from your organization's mission statement and core values. Account administrators should have a thorough understanding of institutional objectives, priorities, and guiding principles, so they can make smart decisions about content that will align with those goals and beliefs and will also be of interest to your target audiences.

Setting Up an Institutional Twitter Account

Signing up for a Twitter account is simple, but you should have a few things worked out before you start the process. Your username, picture, and bio should follow the rules set up in your social media policy. Usernames should be consistent across all social media accounts, but you should have a backup username ready in case the one you want is already taken by another account. (For the record, this is why it's a good idea to set up accounts with your preferred username on popular social media platforms that you are not using now but think you may use in the future.) If your institution's name is trademarked or the username you want seems to belong to an abandoned account, you can report the account to Twitter and ask them to release the username so it is available again for your use, but this can be a time-consuming process and there's no guarantee that Twitter will acquiesce to your request (Nisen 2014).

A username cannot be longer than fifteen characters, can only contain alphanumeric characters and/or underscores, and cannot contain the words "admin" or "Twitter" in it. Try to pick a username that is as close to your actual organization's official name as possible so it's easy for users to recognize who the account represents. Remember that users might tag you in tweets by using your username instead of spelling out your full institutional name, so make sure your username will make sense in this context. (For example, if the College of Staten Island Library's Twitter handle was @csilibrarytweets, instead of @csilibrary, it would sound odd when a user mentions the library in a tweet like "I checked out some great books from @csilibrarytweets today!")

Along with your username, you will need to add a display name, which can be up to fifty characters and can include emojis, non-English characters, and specialized fonts (via websites like Twitter Fonts Generator: lingojam.com/TwitterFonts). You can try to impress users with your tech-savvy by adding special characters or display fonts, but remember also that the account needs to look official and professional. Also, special characters don't always display on all devices or platforms or work well with accessibility tools, so you're risking your display name being read incorrectly by screen-reading software or showing up as the dreaded empty box characters for your users.

An e-mail address can only be associated with one Twitter account, so you cannot use your personal e-mail if you already have a personal Twitter account associated with that e-mail. It is best practice to use an institutional e-mail account when signing up for social media accounts anyway, in case the main contact is away or leaves the organization. If you do not have a general e-mail address that all social media administrators can access, consider creating one just for your social media through a service like Gmail, Inbox, Outlook, ProtonMail, or Yahoo.

If you start following accounts before you have your profile fully set up, complete with profile picture and bio, those accounts are far less likely to follow you back, so after creating your account,

you should add a profile picture right away, even if it's only a temporary one. There are actually two kinds of profile pictures associated with a Twitter account. One is your profile photo, which is displayed next to every update you post and also on your profile page, above your bio. Twitter recommends using a picture that is 400 by 400 pixels in size and supports JPG, PNG, and GIF file formats. When selecting a photo or logo to use as your profile picture, keep in mind that it will be displayed in icon-size (about 48 by 48 pixels, smaller on mobile devices) alongside your posts, so details that may be visible in the larger version may not be clear in the smaller ones. When creating or cropping your chosen image in an image editor like Photoshop or GIMP, try shrinking it down to 50 pixels or so, just to see what it will look like at that size. (You don't need to save the smaller version; Twitter will create it automatically from the picture you upload to your profile.)

The second type of profile picture is the header image, which appears across the top of your Twitter profile. The recommended dimensions for a header image are 1500x500 pixels. Header photos are not required and can be swapped out with just a plain color background. If you do choose to include a header photo, keep in mind that it displays slightly differently on the desktop version of Twitter versus the mobile version and that your profile photo will cover some portion of the lower left-hand side of the image.

Next you will have to create a bio for your institution, describing it in 160 characters or less. When crafting your bio, think of it like an "elevator pitch" for both your organization and your account. You obviously want to mention who you are, but also give people some context for why they should care about your account. Is your archive, library, or museum part of a larger entity or system? Do you have a mission or a focus that you want people to know about? If you plan to tweet about things outside your own collections and events (and we hope this book convinces you to do just that), then what sort of things will you be tweeting about? Although you cannot use HTML in your bio, Twitter will automatically hyperlink any URLs, hashtags, and references to other user accounts that are in the @

username format. Also, URLs with more than thirty characters will be shortened so that they don't take up too many of your limited characters.

REBRANDING AND RELAUNCHING YOUR TWITTER PRESENCE

Twitter has been in existence since 2006, so your organization might easily find itself in the position of having an account that has gone inactive due to employees leaving or changing positions or a perceived lack of interest and interaction on the part of users. Often an account is started up after a motivated employee or manager attends a conference presentation or reads an article that gets them excited about the prospect of better reaching patrons, only to find that maintaining an active and engaging Twitter presence is much more work than some presenters or authors led them to believe.

If you're thinking of relaunching an institutional Twitter account that has stagnated, or if you just want to rebrand an active account that you want to take in a different direction, make sure to involve all original stakeholders in the discussions. Find out why the account was abandoned or why people think it's not working in its current form. Try to assess how successful the institution's Twitter posts were at soliciting engagement and participation within your community. If you have access to event statistics, look beyond interaction on Twitter and check for correlations between outreach efforts and event outcomes. Do highly retweeted posts actually result in increased event attendance or exhibit visitation? Do events or exhibits publicized via Twitter seem to bring in attendees or visitors from specific demographics? Did retweets or interactions from specific accounts boost event participation? You can use this information to work smarter, not harder with your new account by choosing where and when to focus your energy.

If your organization has student workers, volunteers, or interns, ask them about their social media habits. Ask if they follow any corporations, brands, or nonprofit groups and why. What do they expect from a nonpersonal Twitter account? What do they find invasive or annoying? If possible, run a survey for your patrons (you can use online services like Google Forms or SurveyMonkey or even simple paper slips at the Reference and Circulation Desks). Try to get a feel for how many patrons are even using Twitter and what they're using it for. Do they like to hear about local events? Regional news stories? Quotes? Cool pictures? You don't have to build your entire new presence around these things, but you can use the feedback to make the case to your organization that the scope of your posts can go beyond just institutional news and events and find ways to tie in other community information.

Along with user research, it's helpful to do some "competitive" brand research. Identify institutions similar in size, collection(s), purpose, budget, demographics, and so on and check out their social media presence. What are they tweeting about? Do they always include images? Are users interacting with their posts through replies and retweets? Make a list of what seems to be working for those institutions, and let it guide what, how, and when you post.

If you decide to relaunch your institution's Twitter presence with a new Twitter handle/username, you can either switch over the username on your old account, thereby keeping all your old followers and people you follow, or you can start fresh with a new account. If you want to start a brand new account with your old username but keep the old account for archiving purposes, just create a new account with a temporary name, switch your old account over to a different name, and rename the new account with the old username. Make sure to make the transition quickly, as once you release the old username, it will technically be available to other users until you reclaim it on your new account (McGillivray 2014).

REFERENCES

Burkhardt, Andy. "Social Media: A Guide for College and University Libraries." *College and Research Libraries News* 71, no. 1 (2010). crln.acrl.org/index.php/crlnews/article/view/8302/8392.

Ciotti, Gregory. "The Psychology of Color in Marketing and Branding." *Entrepreneur*. April 13, 2016. www.entrepreneur.com/article/233843.

Heinz, Matt. "The 5-3-2 Rule for Social Media Content." *Heinz Marketing Blog.* October 12, 2011. www.heinzmarketing.com/2011/10/the-5-3-2-rule-for-social-media-content.

Lee, Kevan. "How to Find Your Social Media Marketing Voice." *Buffer Social Media Blog.* Revised October 10, 2016. blog.bufferapp.com/social-media-marketing-voice-and-tone.

McGillivray, Erica. "How to Rebrand Your Social Media Accounts." *Moz Blog.* April 3, 2014. moz.com/blog/how-to-rebrand-your-social-media-accounts.

National Archives and Records Administration. "Social Media at National Archives." 2016. www.archives.gov/social-media/strategies.

Nisen, Max. "The Complete Guide to Getting the Twitter Handle You Want." *Quartz.* April 16, 2014. qz.com/197227/complete-guide-to-twitter-handles.

Seiter, Courtney. "20 Great Social Media Voices (And How to Develop Your Own)." *Marketing Land.* August 13, 2012. marketingland.com/20-great-social-media-voices-and-how-to-develop-your-own-18057.

2

Making Connections

If you are just getting started with a new Twitter account, the single most important tip for getting new followers in the beginning is to have a fully completed profile. This means a professional-looking profile picture, a descriptive bio that explains exactly who you are and what you do, a link to your website, and preferably a few tweets under your belt. If you can also find some colleagues or related organizations who you can personally ask for follows, that is extremely helpful as well. This way, when someone views your account, it does not look like a blank slate or abandoned space.

Whom you choose to follow can also influence who follows you. When you start an account, Twitter will often add suggested accounts for you, so the first thing you should do after completing your profile is to weed this list down to only those accounts you think will provide useful information or interaction. Remember that other users can see your following list, so who you are following does say something about your organization. Larger organizations and celebrities are less likely to follow you back, so they are good accounts to follow when you first launch your account. (You'll want to wait until you have a more established presence, meaning more tweets posted and more followers, before you follow accounts that you hope will follow you back. We'll go into this in more detail later in the chapter.)

Once your profile is complete and you are following some accounts and have posted a few times, you can start seeking out individuals and organizations that you'd like to also have as followers. These should be accounts that could be of value in terms of interaction like exchanging useful information and ideas and the ability to retweet your posts to reach a larger audience.

BUILDING A FOLLOWING

There are a few simple ways to gain followers when you're first getting started on Twitter. First, make sure your Twitter link is prominently posted on your website (or at least easily findable, like in the footer or in your main navigation with your other social media links), as well as in any informational or promotional materials. Check to see if your parent or sibling organization(s) has a list of affiliated social media links and request to be added to that list. Make sure to try a search of your site for the keyword "Twitter" to ensure that the top search results will help easily direct users to your Twitter account in the case they can't find the link any other way (Estes, Schade, and Nielsen 2009). The best way to optimize your site search results to include Twitter near the top of the results list is to add your social media accounts to your "Contact Us" page. If your museum has a "Get Involved" page, add your Twitter handle with a list of suggested hashtags for visitors to use when tweeting about the museum. This will also help reinforce to your users that your social media channels are geared toward interaction, not just broadcasting. Adding your social media policy to the policies page on your website and listing your social media accounts

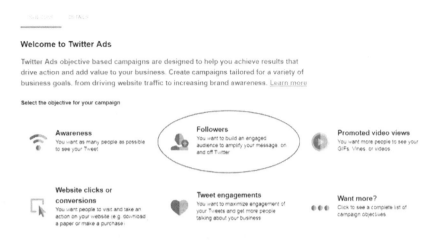

Figure 2.1.   Creating a Twitter Followers campaign.

on your "Publications" page (if you have one) are other ways to draw attention to your Twitter presence. Twitter *is* a publishing platform, after all, and someone browsing your website for annual reports or newsletters might easily stumble upon the link this way. Finally, insert your Twitter link into the template of any e-mail correspondence you send out, like e-newsletters or notifications.

The next step is to find and follow members of your target audience with the hope that they will follow back. You can find potential followers by searching Twitter by location and keyword (more on setting up Twitter advanced searches in the next section) and by looking at the follower lists of similar institutions in your area. As an institution, it's probably best to avoid requesting access to locked accounts (i.e., accounts whose users have set the privacy of their accounts to "protected" so that only users they approve can view their tweets). You want to create a community, but you also want to respect your community's right to privacy, and some people view social media as a way to keep in touch with friends and family and want to restrict their online circles only to people they know, so try to avoid inviting yourself into spaces where you're likely not welcome.

Using Twitter Ads to Promote Your Account

If you have a marketing or social media budget you can use for launching your Twitter presence, you can use Twitter Ads to create a Followers cam-

Figure 2.2.   Setting up your campaign budget.

paign to promote your account to a targeted audience. You can create a Followers campaign by going to ads.twitter.com and clicking on "Followers."

Pricing works through a bidding model, where you bid on how much you're willing to pay for each new follow you receive via the campaign. Usually bids range from ten cents to two dollars, with you paying a lower amount than your maximum bid if you get a higher than average follow rate (Twitter's average campaign follow rate is about 0.1 percent). You can also set a daily and total budget, so the campaign automatically cuts off when you hit a certain cost.

You will then have the option to choose any tweets you want to promote. You don't have to promote individual tweets; you can leave this section blank if you just want to be a "Promoted Account" and have your profile badge show up in people's "Who to Follow" section and have your account prioritized in search results. If you do choose to promote specific tweets, it makes sense to craft a tweet specifically for your campaign, which either highlights an important service, event, or promotion or showcases the kind of content that you think would make your account attractive to your target audience. Promoted tweets will show up in the timelines of your targeted audience (Twitter 2018a).

The next step is to select your audience. You can define a target audience by interests, geography, language, or technology or by selecting other accounts and targeting users similar to their followers. For the latter option, you can choose accounts similar to your own such as other nonprofits or local businesses, regional groups and societies, or other archivists, curators, and librarians. You can also upload custom lists (for example, if you have an e-mail list or sign-up sheet from an event or promotion), or you can put a custom code snippet on your website and target website visitors. Remember that you are going to be paying per follower based on the percentage of people who see your promoted account or tweets and choose to follow you, so you want to tailor your audience as best you can. Cast a wide enough net that many people are seeing your content, but specific enough that there's at least a chance they will be interested in following you.

Note that in Followers campaigns you only pay for "followers," so you don't pay just for people engaging with your content. People can click on or retweet your promoted tweets, click through to your profile, or even click through your website or contact information, and you don't pay for it (Kim 2016).

Twitter Promote Mode

In February 2018, Twitter launched a beta version of a new method of promoting tweets called Twitter Promote Mode. For $99 per month, Twitter will automatically choose tweets from your account to promote on a daily basis, as well as featuring you as a Promoted Account to your target audience. With this option, you can select your target audience, but you cannot choose which tweets to promote (Twitter does the selection for you based on their "quality filter": business.twitter.com/en/help/ads-policies/prohibited-content-policies/Quality_Policy.html). Although this is a bit of a pricey option, it could make sense to budget for a few months' subscription, as Twitter touts an average additional account reach of thirty thousand people, usually resulting in about thirty new followers per month (Twitter 2018b).

SPARKING ENGAGEMENT

Interacting with Users in Your Community

Almost any article or presentation about how organizations should communicate via Twitter will start off by stressing that the platform should not be used solely as a broadcasting channel. In other words, Twitter should be used for two-way communication between an official account and its followers (or potential followers), and not one-way communication aimed at a community or communities. What sometimes gets glossed over in stressing this point is Twitter's strengths regarding the broadcasting of information, namely timeliness and ease of updating.

Quite often institutions will post regularly scheduled content to their Twitter account but fail to optimize its potential as an up-to-the-minute source of news from that organization. It can be very frustrating to your community when "word is going around" that printers are down, the Wi-Fi is not working, or some emergency has affected resources or services, and they cannot find any information about it on your social media accounts. It may be difficult or inefficient to update your website with such information on the fly, and you probably don't want to spam your users with e-mail about what might be a very short-term issue, but posting to Twitter can be done easily and from anywhere. Make sure your account administrators are kept in the know about current issues and that they have the ability and authority to keep your community updated and to respond to questions and concerns about current events and issues in a timely manner.

The ultimate goal of an organization's presence on Twitter, however, is to go beyond just providing information in a passive way. You can create dialogue within your community through both reactive and proactive interaction, where you not only respond to users who refer to you directly in order to answer their questions or solve problems they might be having, but where you also seek out users who need help or who might be interested in your organization's resources or services but are unaware of them. Obviously proactive interaction should be used judiciously, as some users may not be comfortable with unsolicited conversation from someone they don't know. On the other hand, if you are a large, well-known institution or organization, a user might be flattered or find some novelty in your group striking up a conversation with them.

Verified Accounts

If you see a blue checkmark next to an account's name, that means the account has been verified officially by Twitter. This means that Twitter has done their best to certify that the account officially represents the actual person or organization it claims to and that the person or organization is of public interest. As of early 2018, Twitter had suspended the account verification process, but it's likely they'll bring it back in some form in the near future. Public/educational institutions should definitely attempt to get their accounts verified, as it lends credibility and lets your users know that

you are authorized to officially post on behalf of your organization. In order to apply for account verification, you will need to make sure that the e-mail address associated with your account is an official organizational e-mail and that you've gone through the process of verifying your phone number (this basically just means you've added a number to the account; see help.twitter.com/en/managing-your-account/how-to-add-a-phone-number-to-your-account for more information). If you've set up your account as discussed earlier in this chapter, you should be all set to apply for verification. Twitter requires that your username accurately reflect your organization and that you have a properly branded profile and header photo, a completed bio, an accurate location, and a link to your website. When you're ready to apply for the blue checkmark, head over to verification.twitter.com and provide five websites that prove you are who you are (ideally related organizations that link to you) and tell them in five hundred characters or less why you think the account should be verified. This part is obviously up to you, but it helps to go a little beyond your bio or your elevator pitch here and mention why you think your account is of value to your community. What services are you seeking to provide to them via Twitter, and why does it matter that they know they can trust your account? Once you submit your application, Twitter will let you know when they've made a decision regarding your account. If you are turned down on the first try, you can apply again in thirty days (tip: use those thirty days wisely: make sure to ramp up your posting and your interaction!).

Your account administrators should not only keep track of Twitter users who mention your organization by its Twitter handle (these will show up in your mentions feed, and so are fairly easy to monitor), but you should also set up Twitter searches for anyone referring to your organization by name, including any nicknames or common abbreviations. To set up a Twitter search, just go to twitter.com/search-advanced, and add as many search parameters as you need. The advanced search feature also conveniently has a "not" parameter, which allows you to exclude results containing certain search terms. (This is an extremely useful function when

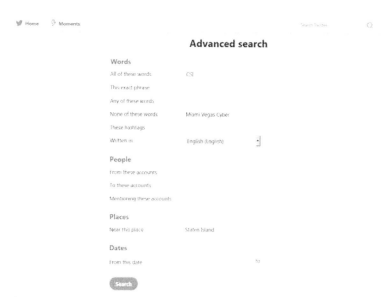

Figure 2.3. Using Twitter's advanced search features.

you work at the College of Staten Island, also known as CSI, and there are many "Crime Scene Investigation" results you don't want cluttering up your search feed.)

You can also set up very general searches for "archive," "library," or "museum" and restrict the location to within a certain distance of your organization, for proactive engagement purposes or to seek out problems or complaints in order to gather honest feedback about your resources and services. The results of your custom searches generate a unique URL, so once you create an advanced search, you can bookmark the results page in order to re-run the search on a regular basis. You can also save your searches as RSS feeds, so that you get automatic updates within your RSS feed reader of choice (like Feedly or Digg Reader). Lifewire has an excellent guide to turning Twitter searches into RSS feeds with services like TwitRSS. me and Queryfeed (Nations 2018). For hacks on building an RSS feed that includes all of Twitter's advanced search parameters or converting advanced search URLs into RSS feed URLs, see the author's *Twitter RSS Feed Creation Cheat Sheet* parts 1 and 2 here: (1) theinfobabe.blogspot.com/2011/06/twitter -rss-feed-creation-cheat-sheet.html (2) theinfobabe .blogspot.com/2012/01/twitter-rss-feed-cheat-sheet -redux.html.

In her chapter "Using Twitter for Research" from the book *Conversations with Visitors: Social Media in Museums*, Beck Tench makes some compelling points for using Twitter searches to monitor the conversations happening around your institution:

> Twitter turns our thoughts, conversations and gut reactions—once a private and closed economy—into open, mineable, collectable goods. Never have we been so intimately connected with our visitors—to know what they think of us alongside what they think of their family, their friends, their dinner. Never have we seen such scale and diversity in what is communicated about us, to us. Never have we been able to command the instant and direct attention of a visitor through an @reply or direct message to their mobile device. More importantly, never has all this been available to us willingly and for free. (2012, 87)

Monitoring your reputation on Twitter isn't just about gathering information. As Tench points out, it enables us to find and interact with patrons online. But why go out of your way to generate interaction on Twitter in the first place? Boosting engagement through interactive content, responding to questions or concerns, and connecting users with other users or accounts that could be of interest to them requires a lot of time and effort on the part of your organization's social media person or team of people. Studies have shown that public engagement via social media gives people a stronger sense of attachment to an organization (Wang, Ki, and Kim 2017), and that the work that goes into establishing and maintaining an active Twitter presence pays off through the growth of social capital within its networks and communities. Social capital is a kind of goodwill that people feel toward others that they are connected with, which makes them more likely to trust, cooperate with, do favors for, and speak on behalf of the other person or entity. It is these strong, positive connections with others in your network that create a solid, engaged community in general and loyal patrons for archives, libraries, and museums specifically.

A big part of earning social capital from patrons in your communities is engaging with them in such a way that they feel as though they have a voice and that their voice is heard. This means not just providing them with an outlet for comment (which Twitter does by default), but also keeping them informed about decision-making processes, responding to their comments and questions in a timely manner, being genuine and not simply responding with repetitious or scripted answers, and letting them know how their comments, criticisms, or suggestions are being addressed.

@MSUArchives

Michigan State University Archives & Historical Collections (twitter.com/MSUArchives/with_re plies) runs an excellent Twitter account that demonstrates how you can interact with your community in a conversational yet professional way. They not only ask questions and reply quickly and frequently. They don't force users who make inquiries through Twitter to go through traditional channels for more information, instead allowing a user to conduct the entire interaction through Twitter or move it to e-mail if the user so desires. They also make a point to promote content shared with them by their users, as well as other local institutions, and to respond to comments that are closed-ended and don't necessarily require acknowledgment (they sometimes use this as an opportunity to share additional information with the user, since they're already showing an interest in the topic). In this exchange: twitter.com/michigansta teu/status/951485396722049024, they not only respond to users who commented on the original image of cows crossing a campus bridge, but they found and shared related photos to add to their responses. Perusing the MSU Archives account is a great way to get inspiration for how to take your interaction and communication skills up a notch.

Because institutions have the potential to reach and interact with a larger and more diverse group of people than the average individual, they also have a wonderful opportunity to make connections and bring people together. Sometimes you are best serving your community not by advertising your own resources or services, but by connecting your followers with other, outside sources. You can do this by recommending other local institutions, connecting users with the heads of appropriate groups or support services, or pointing users to accounts that might be of interest to them based on your own interactions with them. When you are promoting others within your community, like local authors, artists, or civic groups, check to see if they have a professional Twitter presence, and be sure to tag them, as well as linking to their portfolio, website, article, or event information. This allows them to be part of the conversation about them and makes them more likely to join in that conversation, connect with you, and share your posts with their own networks. It also gives them an opportunity to respond directly to other members of your community who have questions or comments and fosters positive feelings toward your organization if it helps increase their own followership, readership, event attendance, or fan base.

Another great way to prompt interaction among your followers is to ask questions aimed at sparking conversation. You can ask them what they like best about your organization or collection or help out users by sharing their requests for recommendations with your larger community (whether they be book recommendations or restaurant recommendations, you can use the opportunity to connect your followers with one another and get them to interact not only with your organization but with each other). Don't just retweet user responses though. It can get repetitive and appear lazy to your followers (Estes, Schade, and

Nielsen 2009). Either just retweet the best responses (with your own comment to add context, preferably), or compile them into a blog post. Make sure to tag users whose responses are included, so they see that their suggestions are being highlighted.

If You're the Expert, Then Act Like It

The Nielsen Norman Group's 2009 "Social Media User Experience" report warns companies not to ask for suggestions on topics that those companies are supposed to be experts on (Estes, Schade, and Nielsen 2009, 110). Their study found that users were annoyed to be getting information from other users on a topic that the company itself was best positioned to give. The *New York Times* (@nytimes) learned this lesson the hard way in 2017, when they asked for recommendations of books written by women on behalf of one of their editors. Users were outraged that a *New York Times* editor, who obviously has access to comprehensive, respectable book reviews and lists, would put the work of finding female authors on users. This seemed like information that should be *coming* from the *New York Times*, not being sought out by them. The *Times* editor in question explained that the account had tweeted his question without context, and the *Times* itself later apologized, but this still serves as a good cautionary tale. It's OK to crowdsource information, and it's great to get feedback from your followers, but make sure you've done and shared your *own* research first. Had the tweet been phrased more along the lines of: "Here's a list of our favorite female authors; who are yours?" it might have been received with a lot less rancor (Zhu 2017).

Interacting with Other Organizations

When looking for other organizations to follow, don't just consider institutions similar to your own. Consider groups with shared or complementary core values (such as museums and colleges, public and special libraries), as well as local businesses or civic groups. Some examples of accounts you should look for, follow, and interact with include:

- Girl and Boy Scouts
- 4-H and garden clubs
- senior-living centers
- tour companies, convention centers, and visitor bureaus
- primary and secondary schools
- living history/re-enactment groups
- sororities and fraternal organizations

Once you start following other accounts, Twitter will also make suggestions to you based on those accounts you already follow. You can also mine the following lists of people or organizations in your area to see who they follow and interact with. Because you are trying to create a community of interaction, rather than just act as a broadcast channel, it is helpful to create a network of connections, rather than just build a large follower base, because you want to generate and be able to follow conversations that are happening in your communities.

There are many ways to interact with institutional accounts that can be mutually beneficial for both groups. The easiest and most common method is to retweet events from other local cultural institutions that might be of interest to your community. For example, if you manage the account for an academic library, sharing information about events or resources at the local public libraries, exhibits at local museums, and appropriate job or volunteer opportunities shows your followers/potential followers that your account is useful beyond just providing information about your own library or school, which they may feel they already know all they need to know about. If you feel the information in the post that you are sharing with your own community is relevant for a particular reason (for example, it could be a lecture or an exhibit on a topic related to a common class assignment or popular course), instead of just retweeting the post, choose "Quote Tweet" instead, and add some context about why you are sharing it. You want your users to feel like you are posting specifically to them as a group, and not just sharing a lot of "noise" that they don't know why they should care about.

Another way to interact with other institutions on Twitter is initiate conversation with them. When users see organizational or business accounts interacting with each other in a casual way, it humanizes the accounts and reminds people that there is a person or people behind the tweets, not just a bureaucratic entity. It makes your account seem more relatable and makes individual users more likely to interact with your account in the future. Often, brands on Twitter interact with each other in a playful way (although sometimes they do take what seems like mean-spirited jabs at each other), usually with the hopes of creating buzz and getting massively retweeted, or going viral. For educational and cultural institutions, the "witty banter" route is certainly an option, but you and your users will get more actual value out of productive conversations. For example, schools can ask museums if there are discounts for students or if local public libraries have museum passes that can be checked out for use. Public libraries can find out if academic library resources can be used by the public. Museums can find libraries with space to do remote exhibits. Obviously all these conversations are already happening between institutions, and partnerships like these are quite common, but having them in public on Twitter gives your users a chance to see those partnerships develop and grow and makes them aware of services and resources they may not have been made aware of via other marketing channels.

Interacting with local businesses can be a trickier task. Nonprofit and/or educational organizations generally do not promote specific companies or commercial endeavors that they are not directly affiliated with. If the business is the proprietor of software or services used by your institution, it's generally fine to promote contests or product launches or upgrades that are aimed at your community because you are paying for that service to provide it to your users, so marketing on their behalf benefits your organization as well. But if you list your location on your profile (which you definitely should do), you may notice that local restaurants and stores start following you with the hopes that they can leverage that connection to market themselves to your user groups. Cross-promotion or interaction with local business is not necessarily off-limits in all cases. For example, local businesses may be sponsoring an event like a street fair or a charity sports game that may be of interest to your community. In that case, you're promoting the event, not the business itself. But no matter what, keep in mind that who you interact with and who you choose to retweet, while not necessarily implying a direct endorsement of them, does in some way color the way in which people will view your organization. We are known

by the friends we keep, and if you often interact with a business that then gets bad press for one reason or another, it can look bad for your organization as well. When it comes to local businesses, if they are offering discounts or promotions that you think would be of benefit to your community, there can be safety in numbers. Consider doing a "roundup" of local eateries for students or a list of stores that give discounts with museum or library memberships or student IDs.

HANDLING NEGATIVE INTERACTIONS PRODUCTIVELY

When you make yourself publicly available on social media platforms, you cannot always predict or control the direction that conversations will take. While sometimes you are aware ahead of time that an event or resource will be controversial, problems can pop up at any time over any matter. It's important to understand that Twitter is not a place where you can hope to completely control the narrative of any story. It belongs to the users, and when you use it, you are interacting with them in their space, not your own, so be respectful of that. One of the main attractions of Twitter is that people feel like it gives them a place where they can openly voice their opinions and concerns, so trying to shut down conversations because you feel they are negative is likely to just make a bad situation worse.

Many organizations are embracing the concept of "radical transparency," or the idea of being open and sincere in online interactions, even if that means admitting to mistakes or having difficult conversations with your community. This method of interaction requires an institution to embrace the humanity behind their online accounts and encourage the people who administer those accounts to really listen to concerns and criticism and to respond thoughtfully and genuinely, rather than just parroting back policy-speak or boilerplate disclaimers. This doesn't mean rushing to respond to negative feedback with the first reaction that comes to you. Take some time to go over possible responses and to research how other organizations have responded to controversy. Try to come up with a few possible directions to take the conversation in, and run those by some coworkers to gauge their reactions. Don't leave the user hanging though; thank them for sharing their thoughts and let them know that you will be addressing their concerns and getting back to them if possible, so they don't feel ignored (Crosby 2010). If you are worried about responding in a way that will have legal ramifications, always be sure to meet with supervisors and/or your organization's legal counsel to make sure you're not admitting to an actionable wrongdoing on the part of your institution. (For example, if someone complains that they injured themselves in your building, apologizing for their injury and admitting that others have been hurt in the same spot or that there have been other complaints about that spot may be admitting to legal wrongdoing and could be used in a suit against your organization. Whenever someone is claiming a physical or severe emotional injury, always bring it to your legal counsel before responding to the complaint.)

Remember that companies regularly pay good money to solicit feedback from their customers, through user testing, focus groups, and free product samples, so an honest opinion from a member of your community is always an opportunity to improve or market your space, collections, or services. No one likes to hear bad things about themselves, but when students at the College of Staten Island complain on social media about problems they're having on campus, it's actually a goldmine of opportunities for the college to make improvements

Using Negative Feedback as an Opportunity for Dialogue

At Clemson University in South Carolina, during the spring 2017 semester, a student tweeted a complaint to the Clemson University Library (@clemsonlibrary) involving the lack of stock in one of their vending machines. Instead of just pushing the student (now students, since another student seconded the complaint) off on another department, the library contacted Dining Services on Twitter (@ClemsonDining), to let them know about the problem. Dining Services promised to remedy the situation. The library then retweeted their response, tagging the original students, much to their delight. It is a great example of inter-organizational interaction on Twitter, as well as radical transparency. Clemson University Library (and Dining Services) took a complaint that easily could have been dealt with behind the scenes—or worse, ignored—and handled it publicly, openly, and with a positive spirit and good sense of humor, and thus turned it into an excellent public relations moment. Even if the impact was relatively small (although who knows how many other students saw the exchange and whose opinions of the library were similarly positively affected), it took only the extra effort of monitoring their Twitter mentions and tagging another department to bring them into the conversation.

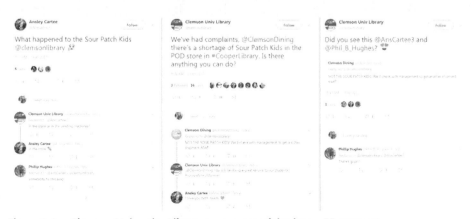

Figure 2.4. Clemson University Library turns a complaint into a PR moment.

where they will be most felt and appreciated and to show the students that they're listening and they care about the obstacles they're facing in class or around campus.

When interacting in online spaces, you should never, in principle, shut down conversation just because it is critical of your organization, but your social media policy should draw a line where harassment or abuse is concerned. If conversation becomes in any way threatening or abusive toward your employees or other members of the community, you should warn the offending user that their behavior violates organizational policy and that if the tweets are not removed, they will be blocked and reported. (Depending on the egregiousness of the post, you may decide to skip the warning and block immediately, so that tweet no longer appears in the thread. Obviously you should use this method judiciously, but threats to anyone's well-being or safety should never be tolerated, and in those cases you should also probably consider contacting local authorities. If you think you may have to call in the authorities, make sure to screenshot the offending tweets before blocking the account.)

The most important thing when dealing with negative comments from your patrons is to maintain a positive attitude. Take all complaints as constructive criticism, even if they are not originally framed that way. You can quickly turn the tone of an interaction from negative to positive just by signaling to the patron that you are listening, you appreciate their feedback, and you're sympathetic to their situation. You won't always be able to resolve every user's issues, and they won't always walk away from the conversation satisfied, but your other patrons (and possibly even the dissatisfied patron, given time) will appreciate that you care about the opinions of your community; are willing to engage in civil, open dialogue; and are committed to ongoing self-assessment and improvement.

REFERENCES

Crosby, Connie. *Effective Blogging for Libraries*. The Tech Set Series, no. 10. New York: Neal-Schuman, 2010.

Estes, Janelle, Amy Schade, and Jakob Nielsen. "Social Media User Experience: Improving Notifications, Messages, and Alerts Sent Through Social Networks and RSS." Nielsen Norman Group. 2009. Accessed January 30, 2018. www.nngroup.com/reports/social media-user-experience.

Kim, Larry. "Why Buy Twitter Followers? 10 Things You Need to Know about Followers Campaigns on Twitter." *Marketing Land*. February 4, 2016. mar ketingland.com/buy-twitter-followers-10-things -need-know-follower-ad-campaigns-twitter-160960.

Nations, Daniel. "How to Create Your Own Twitter RSS Feed." *Lifewire*. Updated January 3, 2018. www .lifewire.com/create-a-twitter-rss-feed-3486601.

Tench, Beck. "Using Twitter for Research." In *Conversations with Visitors: Social Media in Museums*, 74–91. Edinburgh: MuseumsEtc, 2012.

Twitter. "Create a Followers Campaign." *Twitter for Business*. Accessed January 30, 2018. business.twitter.com/ en/help/campaign-setup/create-a-followers-campaign .html.

———. "Twitter Promote Mode Help." *Twitter for Business*. Accessed March 8, 2018. business.twitter.com/ en/help/twitter-promote-mode-help.html.

Wang, Yuan, Eyun-Jung Ki, and Yonghwan Kim. "Exploring the Perceptual and Behavioral Outcomes of Public Engagement on Mobile Phones and Social Media." *International Journal of Strategic Communication* 11, no. 2 (2017): 133–147. doi:10.1080/15531 18X.2017.1280497.

Zhu, Nicole. "A NYT Tweet on Books by Women 'Didn't Play Well.' Here's Why." *Columbia Journalism Review*. August 29, 2017. www.cjr.org/criticism/new -york-times-tweet-women-author.php.

3

Choosing Software

Twitter uses an API, or Application Programming Interface, to allow various kinds of software applications to access some of its data and display it in various ways (Wikipedia 2018). This allows developers to build desktop clients, web browser add-ons, and mobile apps that let you not only access your Twitter account through different interfaces and on different devices, but also add functionality to the basic options available via the regular Twitter web interface, such as scheduling tweets and filtering your timeline.

Two of the popular web-based Twitter clients are TweetDeck and Hootsuite. They both have free versions that allow you to be signed into multiple Twitter accounts at the same time and enable you to create your own customized Twitter dashboard, with columns containing the streams of information you want to see side by side, such as your timeline, mentions, lists, direct messages, and searches.

TWITTER WEB CLIENTS

TweetDeck

TweetDeck (tweetdeck.twitter.com) is owned by Twitter and allows you to grant access to your organization's Twitter account to multiple users without sharing the account password with them. This is a great feature if you have a team of people who all need to monitor and post content to one account. To set up the teams feature in TweetDeck, log into the organizational account and click on "Accounts"

in the left-hand navigation bar. Under "Add a team member," search for the username of the person you would like to add (they will need to have their own Twitter account for you to add them as a team member). Click "Authorize."

Once you are logged into TweetDeck and are linked as a team member to any other accounts you manage, you can customize what columns, or streams of information, you want to monitor. To add a stream, click on the "Add column" (plus-sign) icon in the left-hand navigation bar, and choose the type of column you want to display. Available column options include:

- **Home**: default timeline for specified account (this is the timeline you normally see when you log into a Twitter account)
- **User**: all tweets from a specific user's account
- **Notifications**: notifications for a specified account, including when the account's tweets are retweeted, liked, or mentioned, or when the account has a new follower
- **Search**: the results of a Twitter search for a term or hashtag (you can create a column for an advanced search by starting with a basic search and then using the "filter" icon to the right of the search box)
- **List**: a stream of tweets by users in a list you have previously created (or you can also use this feature to create a new list)
- **Collection**: a shareable timeline of curated tweets created by dragging and dropping tweets from other columns or adding them by URL

- **Activity**: user activity from the accounts you follow, including follows, likes, and retweets by those accounts
- **Likes**: likes from a specified account
- **Messages** (one account): Direct Messages for an account that you are signed into or are a team member of
- **Mentions** (one account): when someone mentions any specified account
- **Followers**: follow activity for a specified account
- **Scheduled**: your scheduled tweets
- **Messages** (all accounts): Direct Messages from all your authorized accounts
- **Mentions** (all accounts): mentions from all accounts you are signed into or are a team member of
- **Trending**: trending topics from a specified account or region
- **Live video**: trending live news and events

When you are managing an institutional Twitter account, it is important to post on a regular basis, or your followers are likely to lose interest and not

Figure 3.1. Scheduling a Tweet in TweetDeck.

pay much attention to your account. Obviously this can become difficult over time as there will be periods when you are away from the office or are busy with other projects or tasks, so most Twitter clients offer a feature that allows you to schedule tweets to post automatically. This also allows you to space tweets out (which is especially important if you have multiple people posting to the same account) and to target important tweets for a time and/or day that analytics show to be a high-impact or high-readership time.

To schedule a tweet in TweetDeck, click on the "New Tweet" icon at the top of the left-hand navigation bar. Compose the tweet as you normally would by entering text and adding any links or images you want to include. Under the text box there is a "Schedule Tweet" button that, when clicked, expands to show a clock and calendar. Enter your desired time and select the date for the tweet to be posted to your account.

You can also schedule a retweet of another user's post by clicking the "Retweet" icon underneath the tweet and then selecting the "Quote Tweet" option. This will open the tweet within your account's "New Tweet" window and give you all the same options as if you were composing a regular tweet. All scheduled tweets will appear in a column to the right of your regular columns, unless you have already added a scheduled tweets column elsewhere in your dashboard. (If the column doesn't automatically appear, just click "Add column" and select "Scheduled.") To edit or cancel a scheduled tweet, use the links at the bottom of the tweet within the "Scheduled" column. Editing a scheduled tweet will reopen the tweet in the compose window, allowing you to change the text of the post; add, delete, or swap the image; and/or change the scheduled time and day of the post.

Hootsuite

Hootsuite (hootsuite.com) is a social media client very similar in appearance to TweetDeck but with the added ability to integrate other social networks besides Twitter, including Facebook, Google+, Instagram, LinkedIn, WordPress, and YouTube. This makes it easy to cross-post content to multiple social media accounts through one dashboard. (Note: the free version of Hootsuite [hootsuite.com/plans/free] allows you to connect up to three accounts/profiles. Each Facebook page or group counts as a separate account. To manage more than three accounts, you will need to upgrade to Hootsuite Professional for $19 per month. Hootsuite also has a Team feature, similar to TweetDeck's, that is only available in their higher-level paid plans.)

Another helpful feature is the ability to assign each social media account to its own separate tab, so it is easy to toggle back and forth between them, and to have a customized set of information streams for each account. You can set up a maximum of twenty tabs in a Hootsuite account. Hootsuite also has a browser extension called Hootlet that allows you to post (or schedule a post) to any of your linked accounts without having to open the Hootsuite dashboard. The browser extension is especially useful for sharing content you come across while surfing the web, and it also includes an optional feature that runs a Twitter search alongside your search engine queries. For advanced users, Hootsuite also offers an app directory with free and premium add-ons that add functionality like image editing and analytics.

TWITTER APPS FOR MOBILE DEVICES

Although many Twitter web clients that allow you to create a dashboard of information streams also have mobile versions, the column-based layout does not easily lend itself to vertically oriented mobile devices. Many users instead opt for Twitter's own mobile app, with fewer features but easier to view, or mobile-focused apps like TweetCaster (iOS and Android; free with ads or $4.99 for Pro version) or Tweetbot (iOS and Mac; $4.99 for iOS app, $9.99 for Mac app).

TweetCaster

TweetCaster is the most popular Twitter mobile app after Twitter's own. After installing the app, you can add accounts by clicking on the gear icon at the bottom of the menu list and tapping "Accounts." If you are using the app to manage multiple accounts,

switching between accounts is not very intuitive; it requires tapping on the active account's profile picture in the menu list but not the actual username (tapping the username will take you to the profile page for that account).

A useful feature in TweetCaster is its granular mute options. You can use their "Zip It" tool by tapping a tweet and clicking on the "(-)" icon along the bottom. Zip It allows you to mute a user, a hashtag, tweets containing certain keywords, or tweets from a specific Twitter client, or some combination of those elements. You can set the mute feature to last an hour, a day, a week, a month, or until you manually unmute it. This can be extremely useful when accounts are live-tweeting an event such as a confer-

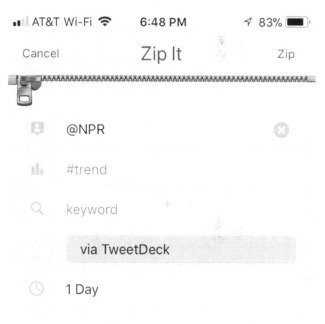

Zip It! Temporarily or permanently mute a person, trend, keyword, or source. Select a zipped tweet at any time to unzip.

Figure 3.2.   Using Zip It in TweetCaster.

ence or during very active Twitter chats. You can temporarily remove tweets from certain accounts that contain the conference or chat hashtag for the duration of the event, without having to unfollow that account.

Although TweetCaster does not have a built-in function to schedule posts, you can connect the app to the service Buffer, which lets you set up a schedule for the dates and times you want your social media posts to go out, and then you just need to add posts to the queue, and they will automatically be sent according to that schedule. Buffer also tracks engagement, so you can adjust your schedule based

on the past performance of your tweets. Buffer also has a function to temporarily suspend auto-posting from your queue, in the event that there is a breaking news story that takes precedence or that might cause certain tweets to seem ill-timed or insensitive.

TweetCaster also includes an enhanced search and list-making functionality with Search Party and SmartLists, as well as built-in photo effects like filters and frames. There is also Instapaper, Read It Later, and Readability integration, so if you use those services to save articles to be read later, you can add tweets to those accounts and then access them from your other devices.

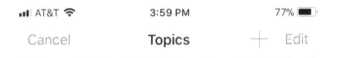

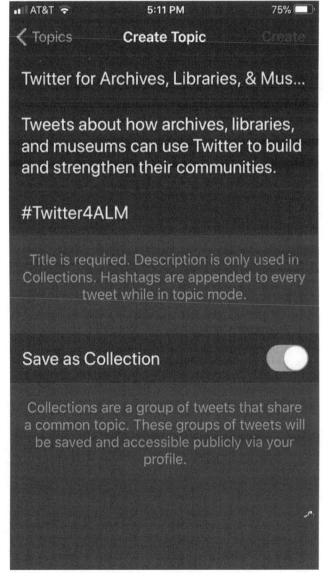

Figure 3.3.   Creating topics in Tweetbot.

Figure 3.4.   Creating topics in Tweetbot.

Tweetbot

Tweetbot, a popular Twitter mobile app for iPhones and iPads, has a corresponding desktop client for the Mac, so you can sync your settings and streams across all your Apple devices. None of the apps has a free version, and there is no Android app, so this software option is mostly for people who have multiple Apple devices and don't mind paying about $20 to install Tweetbot on all of them. Tweetbot has many of the same features as TweetCaster, including multiple account support, granular mute filters, and simple list management, and integrates outside services well into their interface, including bit.ly, CloudApp, Droplr, img.ly, Instapaper, Mobypicture, Pinboard, Pocket, Readability, and yfrog.

As "threading" tweets, or replying to one's own tweet in order for them to be viewed as a linked conversation (sometimes called a "tweetstorm"), has become more popular, Tweetbot has rolled out a handy new feature called Topics. If you want to post multiple tweets on a topic (because your thoughts are longer than one tweet will allow, because you are live-tweeting from an event, or because you want to separate each item into its own tweet but have them be linked together by more than just a hashtag), you can create or choose an existing Topic via the gear icon on the bottom right-hand side of the compose window. Adding a hashtag is optional, so you can add one if you are posting to a Twitter chat or tweeting from an event, but you can leave it out if you just want a regular list of threaded tweets. If you add a tweet to an existing Topic, Tweetbot will automatically thread it after the last tweet in that series. You can also save your Topics as Collections, which then gives you the ability to produce a URL for the string of tweets or to embed them on another site.

One thing some users may have trouble adapting to in Tweetbot is its reliance on "hidden affordances," or possible actions that are invisible or not easily perceived by the user (Borowska 2015), like swiping the screen in a particular direction to make something happen within the app. For example, swiping right on a tweet opens that tweet and any replies, sweeping left on a tweet opens the reply composition window, and a short swipe opens the tweet options, which include the reply, retweet, like, and share options for that tweet. Tapping and hold-ing a tweet opens up the iOS share sheet, which allows you to share or send the tweet to other services (Benjamin 2015). These gesture-based actions can make using the app very quick and easy for expert users but can be very confusing and frustrating for novices, as they're not easy to remember right off the bat and can often be triggered accidentally.

Twitter Mobile App Tips

- When considering mobile apps, each option has its strong suits. Some things to note:
  o Twitter's own app has the most image-editing (and the easiest to use) options.
  o TweetCaster has the best built-in support for cross-posting to Facebook.
  o Tweetbot allows for the most customization, including menu items and gestural navigation.
- Use different apps or always switch back to your personal account if you use one app for personal and organizational accounts, so you don't open up the app to post something personal and accidentally post it to your institution's account. This happens a lot, though it's not always disastrous. For example, an NPR editor accidentally tweeted about his daughter and her love of felines from the official NPR Twitter account, much to the delight of all who witnessed it (Brown 2017).
- None of the Twitter clients we discussed has built-in support for keeping your following/follower lists tidy, so use web services like who.un followed.me and ManageFlitter (manageflitter .com) to manage those lists by removing accounts that unfollow you, are inactive, or are likely spam bots. These services are especially helpful if you're taking the Twitter account over from a previous administrator, so you can analyze and clean up the list of accounts you follow.

SOME NOTES ON CHOOSING TWITTER CLIENTS

Remember that software is just a tool to facilitate a task or tasks. There is no panacea that will work in all situations for all organizations. Here are some things to think about when you are deciding which applications you want to use for managing your institution's Twitter account:

- *Your time is important.* Don't worry about knowing about every single Twitter software option or every single feature and function within the software that you choose. The time it takes you to research and implement a new tool, or to learn how to use a new feature in the software you're currently using, is only worth it if it will save you time and stress in the future. Likewise, your time has worth, so free software is not always the best value for your money. The premium versions of web or mobile apps, or paid add-ons, can in some cases save you money in the future by streamlining your workflow and thus saving you considerable time or preventing you from having to buy other, more expensive software or services like image editing or statistical and analytics packages.

- *Think about software in terms of workflows.* What can combine separate platforms into one, so that you can get more done in one place? But also understand that software that tries to do many things tends to do each one of those things less well than software that focuses on just that one thing. So consider carefully where compromises can be made and where they really can't. Also, what works for you may not work as well for your other team members, so make sure there is consistency with tweets sent from different platforms or applications. Consider creating a sandbox account to test out new software or features before using them on your live account so that you know how the resulting tweets display and you can make educated decisions about whether you want to use them (or allow their use by other social media team members) and whether that functionality adds or detracts from cross-platform posting of various kinds of media.

- *Match the tool to the need.* While it can save you time and energy to find a Twitter platform that allows you to combine tasks that normally would require different tools to accomplish, that doesn't mean you should look for a solution that will do everything. You should always think about your needs first and find the software that suits those needs, instead of just picking a tool with a lot of bells and whistles and forcing yourself to use every available feature just because it's there. At some point, extra functionality just makes software harder to use and hurts your ability to do basic tasks, so sometimes choosing a simple, user-friendly interface is actually preferable to choosing a more advanced platform that adds options you don't really need at the expense of ease of use for the fundamental tasks that make up the majority of your Twitter experience. In other words, use the tools you like and that you are comfortable with. A positive user experience on your part is extremely important to helping you keep your Twitter presence active and vibrant.

REFERENCES

Benjamin, Jeff. "10 Tweetbot Tips for Power Users." *iDownloadBlog.com (iDB)*. October 11, 2015. www .idownloadblog.com/2015/10/11/10-tweetbot-tips -for-power-users.

Borowska, Paula. "6 Types of Digital Affordance That Impact Your UX." *WebdesignerDepot*. April 7, 2015. www.webdesignerdepot.com/2015/04/6-types-of-dig ital-affordance-that-impact-your-ux.

Brown, Tanya Ballard. "That Time #Ramona Made Everyone Smile for a Few Minutes." *NPR: The Two-Way*. October 3, 2017. www.npr.org/sections/ thetwo-way/2017/10/03/555316521/that-time-ra mona-made-everyone-smile-for-a-few-minutes.

Wikipedia. "Application Programming Interface." *Wikipedia*. Accessed February 1, 2018. en.wikipedia.org/ wiki/Application_programming_interface.

4

Curating Content

You may have sent out a few tweets while you were still tweaking your profile, finding and following relevant accounts, and testing Twitter clients, but at some point you should try to settle into a schedule of posting pretty regularly. Don't worry too much about posting an exact number of tweets every day or every week, but you should aim to post about once a day, and when that's not possible, try not to slip below a few posts per week. Your followers will start to notice if you're just trying to meet a quota, however, so sometimes it's better to skip a post or two than to force it by posting too many retweets in a row, content that contains typos or incorrect information or broken links, or content that bears no clear relation to your organization or industry.

Your social media policy, as discussed in chapter 1, should outline some key elements that help you decide what kinds of posts you want to tweet from your institutional account. You obviously want to use social media to promote upcoming events, new resources and services, updated hours or policies, as well as highlight collections, departments, and staff accomplishments, but this will not generally provide enough content to post on a regular basis, so this is where your target audience, as defined in your social media plan, becomes extremely important. You can add immense value for your users if you branch out beyond internal news and information, to also help keep your community informed about other issues that might be of interest to them. For example, an academic library can tweet about lectures or exhibits near campus that relate to coursework or curricula

at its own institution. Archives and museums might want to share online resources that relate to or expand upon the subjects in their own collections. A public library can consider any local events of a civic or educational nature fair game to inform its own Twitter community about.

CRAFTING THE PERFECT TWEET

Writing for Social Media

OK, so there probably is no such thing as "the perfect tweet," but there are definitely ways to make your posts easier to notice, find, and read. Writing specifically for Twitter is tricky business. Best practices for writing in general, or even best practices for writing for the web, don't always apply. For example, writers are often told to use the active voice whenever possible, since it's easier for readers to process information that is presented in a linear fashion. In a tweet, however, you have only 280 characters to get your point across, and users are often scanning a timeline crammed with other tweets that are competing for their attention, so the first few words of your tweet are extremely important. Go ahead and give yourself a pass on the active voice rule whenever it means pushing the most important information to the end of your first sentence rather than the beginning (Nielsen 2007). For example, when using active voice, many of your tweets will begin with "The Museum is/has/will be . . ." Whatever actual information you want to share will then be buried at the end of the sentence.

Users can see your logo/icon and account name, so they can pretty quickly identify who the information is coming from without needing it right at the beginning of the sentence. This frees you up to front-load the sentence with something that might catch their attention, like "Monet's never-before-seen paintings will be featured tonight at the Museum!" Another grammar rule you can ignore pretty freely in Twitter is the use of complete sentences rather than sentence fragments. For example, you could also have written the above tweet as "Monet's never-before-seen paintings: tonight at the Museum!"

Tips for Writing for Twitter:

- Be concise. Break long sentences into shorter, punchier ones or even sentence fragments. Only use adjectives and adverbs that are necessary to make your point.
- Don't repeat your username or full organizational name in the tweet. This takes up precious characters to give users information that is already included by default in every tweet.
- THERE'S NO NEED TO YELL. Use sentence case in your tweets, or title case for headlines or titles, but don't hit that caps-lock key unless it is A VERY BIG EMERGENCY, or else your followers will feel like you're just shouting everything at them.
- Use numerals instead of spelling out numbers. Numeric characters break up text and can help catch the eye.
- If your tweet includes a link, make it clear where the link will take users. Because Twitter automatically truncates long links (and sometimes posters themselves use link-shortening services like bitly or TinyURL), it's not always clear where the user is being directed when they click on a link included in a tweet. Don't just use generic information like "Check out our latest article!" or "Take today's quiz!" Also make sure to indicate if the link will open something other than a regular web page, such as a pdf or a video.
- Proofread, proofread, proofread! Twitter has an of-the-moment feel that can get users in the habit of firing off tweets quickly, without reading them over closely. While this might be fine for a personal account, your organization will quickly

lose credibility if your tweets contain numerous misspellings or grammar errors.
- And speaking of credibility, use text-speak sparingly ("u" for "you," "r" for "are," etc., or emoticons in place of words). There may be times when you absolutely need to resort to an abbreviation or emoticon for space issues (although you have 280 characters now so this should happen far less often) or times when you are purposely assuming a certain voice to match the intended tone of your tweet, but don't overuse these conventions. (Estes, Schade, and Nielsen 2009; HHS 2016)

Using Hashtags

Some other elements that will help your tweet get noticed are hashtags, user tags, images, and/or links. Hashtags serve as keywords that not only help your tweets show up in relevant searches, but they also appear in a different font color than plain text, so they can help draw attention to your tweet. But don't get carried away. Don't use more than three hashtags in one tweet, and always research the "official" hashtags for topics or events rather than just guessing at them. There is no one definitive tool for curating hashtags, but there are hashtag search engines that will show you the popularity of specific hashtags so you can find the most popular one or two for your tweet (try hashtagify, RiteTag, and Keyhole, for example). Usually, it's fine to just use Twitter's native search function to see if a specific hashtag has recent tweets associated with it and if those tweets are on the same topic you are tweeting about. (Alternately, you can just do a keyword or phrase search and see what hashtags others tweeting about that topic or event are using.)

When using hashtags, you also have the choice of working them directly into the wording of your tweet (for example, "It's #BannedBooksWeek at the library!") or listing them at the end of the tweet. If you decide to use a hashtag in the text, make sure it's understandable. If the hashtag is a phrase, rather

Nancy Pelosi ✓ @NancyPelosi · Jan 10

Thanks to the brave women of the #MeToo 🙋 movement, we are at a watershed moment in the fight against sexual harassment. Know that we are with you every step of the way. #TimesUp 👊

Figure 4.1. Hashtags with image icons.

than a word or acronym, capitalizing the first letter of each word makes it more readable (visually as well as with screen-reader software). But keep in mind, the longer the phrase, the harder it will be for your users to make sense of it. Also, sometimes Twitter assigns image icons to popular or trending topics or events, so consider whether that will hurt the clarity of your tweet and consider relegating those hashtags to the end of the tweet.

Archives Hashtag Party

In August 2017, the National Archives (U.S.) started a Twitter campaign aimed at "enabling all types of archives to share their collections on social media around a fun topic" (National Archives 2018). At the beginning of every month, they choose a theme and turn it into a hashtag that other archives can use to post items from their collections that relate to the theme. They also maintain a list of archives who are participating at www.archives.gov/campaigns/archives-hashtag-party-participants. This is a great example of a large institution reaching out and helping give smaller organizations a wider audience.

Tagging Other User Accounts

We mentioned earlier that directly tagging other accounts can help increase interaction by drawing the attention of those accounts, but use discretion when deciding who and how to tag in your tweets. Sometimes an account's username does not make it easy for another user to quickly identify the person, organization, or brand behind the username. When this is the case, use the actual name within the main text of your tweet, and tag the account at the end of the tweet or by tagging the image if you are including one. Figure 4.2 is an example of a tweet using account tags within the text that probably don't make sense to most users. The first is an acronym for the New York State Society of Certified Public Accountants, which is obviously a lot of characters to use up in one tweet but could easily be shortened to NY State Society of CPAs, possibly with the user account tagged in parentheses afterward: "NY State Society of CPAs (@NYS-SCPA)." The second user account tagged is @csinews,

Figure 4.2.   Some usernames can make a tweet hard to understand when they are used in place of the actual name of the person or organization.

which is actually the main Twitter account for the College of Staten Island, but because of the word "news" in the account name, it sounds confusing in a sentence. For followers who know that @csinews is the username for the College of Staten Island, they may just replace the tag in their head with the name of the school while reading, but for anyone else it just makes the sentence fairly nonsensical.

Adding Images to Your Tweets

Images are another great way to draw attention to your tweets. Images can display differently depending on the application being used to access Twitter, but the recommended dimensions for inline graphics is 1200 by 675 pixels (and no smaller than 506 by 253 pixels). You can post a picture of any size or shape, as long as the file size is under five megabytes, but some Twitter clients will crop it to a smaller, 16:9 ratio rectangle when viewed in-stream, and a user will have to click on the image to see the full, uncropped version (Lee 2017). For images outside the 16:9 ratio, or in portrait orientation (vertical rather than horizontally flipped pictures), Twitter tries to "intelligently" crop the image by looking for clusters of objects or dominant features like faces (Vincent 2018). Be careful, though, since Twitter doesn't always get it right, and if it decides to show only the middle portion of an image of two people standing side by side, for example, the picture will make no sense and can be unappealing to users. In this case, consider cropping the picture around the faces, or set up a test account where you can send out tweets to see what they will look like in the wild before posting them to your official account. (Note: if you are using Twitter Ads to create promoted tweets, there are alternative options for image sizing. Please see Twitter Business's "Advertiser Card Specifications" for details: business.twitter.com/en/help/campaign-setup/advertiser-card-specifications.html.)

You can attach up to four pictures to a tweet. When viewed via the Twitter website they will be put into a grid, as follows:

- two images: each 252 by 252 pixels, side by side
- three images: first image will be 337 by 337 pixels, with the other two stacked to the right of it, at 167 by 167 pixels each
- four images: first image will be 379 by 379 pixels, with the other three stacked to the right of it, at 125 by 125 pixels each (Lee 2017)

Other Twitter clients stack images in different ways. For example, Tweetbot, the Hootsuite web client, and Twitter's mobile app always give all images the same width. So two images will split the space 50/50, while three images will put the first image on the left, taking up 50 percent of the space, and then the other two images will be stacked on the right. Four images will be stacked two by two, all the same size. Hootsuite's mobile version uses these same specifications except in the case of three pictures, in which the first two pictures take up the top half of the allotted space, 50/50, and the third picture spans the entire bottom half of the space. Tweetcaster, on the other hand, takes a much simpler route by just cropping each image into a square icon of the same size no matter how many there are and putting them in a row.

Obviously you can't account for all the ways your users might be viewing your images, so how do you decide the best size and shape of your images when you're posting multiples? User testing can give you an idea of the dominant Twitter applications in use by your followers, so you can familiarize yourself with the layouts for those particular applications, but even so, many users are likely to be viewing Twitter regularly on both a web client and a mobile client, which makes it hard to optimize images even then. One solution is to turn your images into a collage, so you can control the proportions of each image in the set. There are many applications for creating picture collages, such as Canva (Android, iOS, and web), Layout (Android and iOS), Pic-Collage (Android, iOS, and Windows), and PicLab (Android and iOS).

Including Links in Your Tweets

Finally, whenever possible you should link your followers to the source of the information you're tweeting about, a place where they can get more information, or further resources. Links are important for sharing purposes, as your followers might want to send the information to friends or colleagues who don't use Twitter, or they might want to repurpose the information on a different social media site or other medium. When you add a link to a tweet, Twitter will attempt to pull an image from that link, so it can also add some visual emphasis to your post. Most major websites have Twitter cards set up on their end, so that Twitter can include an image and page summary with the tweeted link, which can look a lot like if you had added your own image to a tweet, as discussed in the previous section. The difference is that when users click on the image, instead of just getting the full-size version of the image, they will be taken directly to the URL in the tweet. The downsides of this method are that (1) you can't choose the image (unless you are an administrator of the site you are linking to), and (2) not every site has Twitter cards enabled on their end. If Twitter cards are not enabled, users will see just a plain text link.

To set up Twitter cards for your own site, read the "Optimize Tweets with Cards" guide on the Twitter Developers website: developer.twitter.com/en/docs/tweets/optimize-with-cards/overview/abouts-cards. Note:

- You can choose between a summary card, which will include a small icon image or logo, with the summary alongside; a large image with summary beneath; an app card (which includes an app download link); or a player card (which allows videos to be played directly in a Twitter stream).
- Some content management systems and blogging platforms (including Blogger, Tumblr, and WordPress) have Twitter card support built in or have available plug-ins that you can install that will automatically enable cards and choose the most suitable card type for a page or post.

- If you have Twitter cards enabled on your site, but a user includes an image along with your link, the image will take precedence and appear instead of your card.
- If a user tweets multiple links, only the first URL's card will be shown with the tweet. (Twitter 2018c)

Figure 4.3. Examples of a summary card and a summary with large image card.

Figure 4.4. Examples of a summary card and a summary with large image card.

Crafting "Retweetable" Posts

The main goal of your organization's Twitter account should be to keep your own community connected and informed, but when your posts get retweeted by other accounts, it broadens your reach and helps not only to draw in new members to your circle but to connect your community with other relevant groups and organizations.

- Use relevant hashtags so that your tweet is easily findable.
- Tag related accounts, either in the text of the tweet or by tagging an attached image.
- Avoid time-restrictive phrasing like "tomorrow" or "next week." (Use dates if you have to, since they remain relevant the month, week, or day before the event.)
- Create or choose an eye-catching, descriptive visual that is formatted to display well in a Twitter user's feed.
- If multiple sources exist to convey the information you want to share, carefully choose the best one to link to (i.e., from a respected source, with the best summary of information, most appealing images, least obtrusive ads, etc.).
- Use your 280 characters wisely. Users are likely to skim right past a large block of text, but the extra character count now afforded to you allows you to use white space to make details like date, time, and location really stand out. (Related: just because you have 280 characters available, doesn't mean you should use them in every tweet. If you want your visuals to really stand out, or if you think people will want to add their own comments to the tweet when sharing it, keep the text brief.)

USING MEDIA IN YOUR POSTS

We discussed earlier in the previous section that the ideal tweet will usually include an image or other form of media. There are many options for adding media to your tweets, as well as tools for creating graphics specifically formatted to display well in a Twitter feed.

You can easily create images formatted for Twitter with websites and apps like Canva, Pablo (web), or DesignLab Studio (iOS). Each of these programs allows you to select templates preformatted in Twitter's preferred 16:9 or 2:1 ratios and has many options for backgrounds, fonts, and artwork that you can add to the image. Since the templates do most of the design work for you, you can make graphics for events and announcements, or to display quotes for popular hashtags like #MondayMotivation or #Wednesday Wisdom, in next to no time at all.

Another great way to add images to your posts is to share your Instagram photos on Twitter. But don't just auto-post directly from the Instagram app because when the tweet appears on Twitter, the image will not be attached and will instead just include a link to the image. Even though it's a little more work, it's best practice to save the image and post it directly to Twitter with the description and the link to the Instagram post. Unfortunately, you cannot save/download an Instagram photo directly from the Instagram website or app by right-clicking or using the "save image" feature on your mobile device. There are, however, several ways to save an Instagram photo so you can add it directly to a tweet.

- If you posted the photo to Instagram yourself, Instagram should save the photo automatically to your phone. (iOS and Android both automatically create an Instagram album when you use the app on your mobile device, so you can easily find all your Instagram photos in one place. Keep in mind, however, that if you delete the photo from your main camera roll, it will also delete it from the Instagram album.)
- If you are on a desktop computer, you can get a direct link to the photo by right-clicking on the photo in Instagram and selecting "View page source." Scroll down to the part that reads "meta property="og:image"" and copy the link in quotes after "content=." This is the location of the actual .jpg photo file, which you can then open in a new window and right-click to save the photo.
- On a desktop computer or any modern smartphone or tablet, you can take a screenshot of the image. Although the default resolution for screenshots is only 72 dpi, they display well on most personal computer monitors. (However, because of the low resolution, this method may not work so well for images that will be shown on large format displays like those used for digital signage or images that you might want to

include in a print publication like a newsletter or annual report.)

- There are many websites and apps that you can use to download an Instagram photo. The website DownloadGram allows you to paste in the URL of any Instagram photo, and it will create a download link to save a full-size copy of the .jpg file of the photo. For Android devices, BatchSave, FastSave, and QuickSave are just a few of the popular apps for saving pictures from the Instagram app. For iOS, try Repost or InstaSave. (Both apps will include a watermark with the original poster's username on the downloaded photo unless you purchase the Pro versions of the apps. In some cases, it's good to have your photos watermarked so that you will get credit if the picture gets shared without attribution, but occasionally the watermark can get in the way or distract from the photo.)
- If you are using a third-party application to manage your social media, there are some ways to set up your account to include Instagram photos in the auto-posted tweet by default. For more information on cross-posting content from different social media accounts, see chapter 5: "Automating Your Feed."

A perhaps undue emphasis has been placed on users' preference for video content (Strohl 2017). Videos definitely work for drawing attention to a tweet, but not all users want to or can watch and listen to a video at the moment they come across it. They may be at work or school and not have access to headphones or be in a meeting or on public transportation. They may have a hearing impairment or have trouble following dialogue that moves too fast or is not clearly enunciated. This doesn't mean you shouldn't use video with your tweets; it just means that you should supplement your video with as much text description as possible and create or share

Figure 4.5. Finding the direct URL to an Instagram image in their website page source code.

mostly videos that are closed captioned or at least have some form of subtitles.

There are many ways to create and share videos on Twitter. On Twitter's mobile app, you can record and edit video directly from the "compose tweet" window, by clicking on the camera icon and then selecting the red video icon. Press and hold the button to record. You can stop and restart the video to add more shots, up to a total length of two minutes and twenty seconds. If you have multiple clips, you can rearrange or delete individual clips and preview the video before tweeting or making more edits. You can also upload video to Twitter from either your mobile device or your computer. Twitter supports MP4 and MOV files up to 512MB. The maximum video length is still 2:20, but you will have the option to trim the video if it is longer than that (Twitter 2018b).

Twitter uses the live video streaming platform Periscope (www.pscp.tv/, Android and iOS) to allow users to broadcast live video via Twitter. To start a live video on Twitter, click the "compose tweet" icon and then hit the live video button, located next to the camera button. (Don't worry: just clicking the button won't start a live stream right away! After your video stream initializes, you'll see a "Go LIVE" button to actually start your live stream.) Any videos you live stream on Twitter will also be available on Periscope, and if you enable location tagging on the tweet, the video will also be added to Periscope's Global Map discovery tool. When you are finished with your live video, Twitter will give you an option to save a recording of it to your mobile device's camera roll (Twitter 2018a).

If you tweet a video from a website or blog, the way the video displays will depend on how the site owners have set up the Twitter cards for that page. If they have enabled the Twitter video player card, the video will display and play directly in a user's Twitter feed. Some sites just use summary cards for their whole site, whether an individual page features a video or not. In this case, the video will appear as a screenshot image, and when a user clicks on it, it will open the link to the page containing the video on the original site. Currently, YouTube and Vimeo videos appear as small summary cards on the web, but clicking on them opens a larger player that allows the user to watch the video directly in their feed. On mobile apps, videos will open in a new window.

There are many apps and programs for creating videos to share on Twitter or other social media sites. Adobe Spark Video (spark.adobe.com/about/video; web and iOS), Animoto (animoto.com; web, Android, and iOS), Biteable (biteable.com; web), and Magisto (www.magisto.com; web, Android, and iOS) are all easy-to-use tools that allow you to create and edit videos, as well as make slideshows that mix videos, still images, and graphics. If you want to create simple tutorials or screencasts, Jing (www.techsmith.com/jing-tool.html), Screencast-O-Matic (screencast-o-matic.com), and Screencastify (www.screencastify.com) let you capture, record, and share your computer screen. Mobile apps Hype Type (iOS), VideoShow (Android), and Vont (iOS) make it easy to add text to your videos. Those are just some of the ever-growing list of options for creating and editing videos, video collages, slideshows, and more. Just search the web or app store on your mobile device and you can find innumerable websites and apps that let you add filters, music, stickers, and other graphics to enhance your videos.

Another option for adding media to your tweets is animated gifs. In fact, if you have a short video that doesn't require sound, it can make sense to convert it to an animated gif, which doesn't require a special player to view. There are many online tools to convert video to animated gif format like animated gif search engine and host site Giphy (giphy.com), as well as many graphics programs that will work for this purpose such as Adobe Photoshop and Techsmith's Camtasia. If you are a Tumblr user, their app also allows you to create animated gifs from videos, but note that if you post the gif to Twitter from the Tumblr app, it will appear as a still image that links to the Tumblr page. Instead of cross-posting, you might want to just save the gif to your camera roll and post it directly from your preferred Twitter app, so it appears as an animated gif directly in a user's Twitter feed. There are many other mobile apps that will allow you to make animated gifs out of a video or a series of photos (like a photo burst). Giffer (iOS) allows you to create your gif and post it to Twitter directly from their app, and gifs posted from the app will display directly in a Twitter feed.

@AMNH

The American Museum of Natural History makes particularly good use of media in their tweets, including vibrant pictures, animated gifs, and live broadcasts of museum events and behind-the-scenes footage. They pair these with current events like March Madness and popular hashtags like #TBT (throwback Thursday, where you post an old picture or just a memory from a few years back) to help them show up prominently in searches and to engage users to interact.

Figure 4.6.　American Museum of Natural History making use of a popular event (March Madness) to increase visibility and engagement.

If you want to tweet something that you don't have an associated image for, and you don't want to create a graphic specifically for that post, Twitter's built-in animated gif search engine is a great option. When you open the window to compose a tweet, just click the "GIF" button and it will bring up a menu of commonly searched terms and gifs that fall into those categories, or you can use the search box to find something different or more specific. Using animated gifs to express an emotion or reaction is a great way to add a little personality and humor into your Twitter feed.

RETWEETING OTHER ACCOUNTS

Because for most organizations original content will be hard to come up with on a daily basis, you often have to rely on retweeting other accounts to keep your own account active. When selecting content about news, events, or resources that are not technically affiliated with your organization to retweet from your own account, you do need to keep a few things in mind:

1. *Do your research.* If the tweet is about breaking news or information, do a quick Internet search to make sure the content is accurate, even if the tweet is from a well-respected account. Don't just jump on the bandwagon and help spread misinformation. Click on any links included in the tweet, and make sure they work properly and are not sending you through an intermediary portal that makes it more difficult for users to get to the content they're looking for (Google Amp links, for example, rather than direct links to newspaper and magazine articles). At least skim the article or other content being linked to so you're making an informed decision about exactly what information you're sharing. If the tweet has replies, give them a quick skim, so you can see what other users are saying about the tweet. This can alert you to red flags in terms of possibly offensive or even just controversial content, so you can be prepared if your followers have questions or concerns about the tweet. If there are multiple sources tweeting about a topic, take the time to find the best source. (Hint: it's not always the one with the most retweets. Which one is the most researched? Has the most appealing graphic? Uses appropriate hashtags? Is most suited to your own audience? Comes from a source your users might know and respect?)

2. *Understand your users.* This may require setting up focus groups or conducting surveys to define your audience. (Is it mostly students or professors? Democrats or Republicans? What is the dominant age range?) Getting an idea of who your users are doesn't mean you have to cater to a specific demographic or pander to a spe-

cific group or mind-set, but you don't want to alienate your users either. For example, Internet memes are often used on Twitter but may not make much sense to users who do not spend as much time on the Internet as someone who has a smartphone or uses the Internet at work all day. (Note: you should always avoid culturally insensitive language, but it's sometimes easy to slip up and use a common turn of phrase or otherwise say or share something that you don't realize is inappropriate. Knowing your audience and therefore the religious and cultural communities that your institution serves, you can research appropriate terminology and language, as well as learn about common issues and stereotypes faced by those communities, and thus avoid unintentionally causing offense.)

3. *Remember that it's not about you.* Be honest with yourself about what your community is interested in. You can push the boundaries of that, but overall if you're posting mostly things *you think* they should read, and not what they actually *want* to read, they will start to ignore you. Remember, it's about them not you, so you have to lean toward their actual interests and mix in the rest sparsely. As an educational institution, it can often be hard to strike a fair balance between keeping your users educated and keeping them entertained. You might often see news or events that you think your users should know about, but if they genuinely have no interest in that information, they will pass right over it, and every time that happens, you will lose a little bit of clout. Save up your social capital for the really important stuff.

4. *Consider adding context.* When you're retweeting something, remember that whoever originally posted that tweet was considering their own target audience and not necessarily yours. If you have a very similar target audience, a simple retweet may suffice, but if not, quote the tweet instead and add a comment that explains why it might be of interest to your users. Sometimes it makes more sense to not retweet a post at all, but to craft your own tweet on the topic and mention the original poster as a "ht" or "h/t" (hat tip) or by using "via" (e.g., /via @csilibrary).

You would likely choose this method in cases where you want to share the general information, but you feel that you have a better image or link to share than the original post uses (or their image or link is broken or incorrect), or in cases where you want to use entirely different wording, hashtags, and/or user tags.

5. *Curate lists.* Twitter allows you to create lists of accounts, and you can then view a feed of tweets specifically from those accounts. This allows you to curate lists of colleagues, other departments in your organization, similar institutions to your own, popular news sources, nonprofits who might provide services to your community, local civic organizations, and so on, giving you a fast and easy way to find suitable content to retweet. You do not need to be following an account to add them to a list, so lists are also an easy way of keeping your main feed uncluttered, while still having access to specific streams of information you might be looking for at any particular time. If you are a department in a larger institution or system, like a university's archives, or a branch library, having lists of the other departments and other branches allows you to find content from departments and branches with lower follower counts than yours and share their tweets with a wider audience, creating goodwill among units and providing content to your followers that they might not have otherwise come across (as well as letting them know about other accounts they might be interested in!).

6. *Hit the mute button.* Mute accounts to minimize the chance of posting offensive content. Periodically, the main account administrator should go through and mute accounts that shouldn't be retweeted because they post questionable content or have questionable profiles. This is especially important if you have multiple people tweeting from the same account and want to help prevent another user from accidentally retweeting a post from a user with a profile or feed containing what might be considered offensive content. Accounts that just contain the occasional profanity or nudity likely do not warrant blocking them, but if you retweet a post from one of those accounts and

your followers click back to the original poster (the "op" in Internet parlance), your organization can look less professional by association. (Don't worry: you will see interactions in your "Notifications" or "Mentions" feeds even if you have accounts muted, so you won't miss a question or comment from a muted user.)

REFERENCES

Estes, Janelle, Amy Schade, and Jakob Nielsen. "Social Media User Experience: Improving Notifications, Messages, and Alerts Sent Through Social Networks and RSS." Nielsen Norman Group. 2009. Accessed January 30, 2018. www.nngroup.com/reports/social -media-user-experience.

Lee, Kevan. "The Ideal Image Sizes for Your Social Media Posts: Guidelines for All 6 Major Social Networks." *Buffer Social Media Blog.* Last updated December 4, 2017. blog.bufferapp.com/ideal-image -sizes-social-media-posts.

National Archives. "Archives Hashtag Party." Archives .gov. Last updated February 27, 2018. www.archives .gov/campaigns/archives-hashtag-party.

Nielsen, Jakob. "Passive Voice Is Redeemed for Web Headings." Nielsen Norman Group. October 22, 2007. www.nngroup.com/articles/passive-voice-is-re deemed-for-web.

Strohl, Carrie. "The Misleading Debate over Text 'versus' Video." *Viddler Blog.* April 25, 2017. www.viddler .com/blog/misleading-debate-text-versus-video.

Twitter. "How to Create Live Videos on Twitter." Twitter. Accessed January 28, 2018. help.twitter.com/en/ using-twitter/twitter-live.

———. "How to Share and Watch Video on Twitter." Twitter. Accessed January 28, 2018. help.twitter .com/en/using-twitter/twitter-videos.

———. "Optimize Tweets with Cards." Twitter. Accessed February 2, 2018. developer.twitter.com/en/docs/ tweets/optimize-with-cards/overview/abouts-cards.

U.S. Department of Health and Human Services' (HHS) Office of the Assistant Secretary for Public Affairs. "Writing for the Web." Usability.gov. 2016. Accessed February 1, 2018. www.usability.gov/how-to-and -tools/methods/writing-for-the-web.html.

Vincent, James. "Twitter is Using Machine Learning to Crop Photos to the Most Interesting Part." *The Verge.* January 25, 2018. www.theverge.com/2018/ 1/25/16931632/twitter-machine-learning-auto-image -cropping.

5

Automating Your Feed

Your organization's success on Twitter depends on how well the feed engages with your community. We have discussed in previous chapters about building your social media strategy, creating a strategy on gaining followers, and catering your feed's content to keep your followers engaged. As you gain followers and as you curate your content, you want to make sure that your feed engages and performs well with your community. Keeping an original and active feed of content that meets the needs of your community is the key to having a successful Twitter presence. Executing this properly means that you are keeping your followers interested. You want your feed to go beyond the broadcast of different events and services that your organization has to offer. You don't want to be active on Twitter just for the sake of tweeting something every day. You want your posts to connect with your users and have them engage with your organization. For most people that deal with Twitter accounts, it is not the only job that you hold within your organization. Some organizations may have dedicated marketing departments and still need to utilize the concept of automation. Automation can be a lifesaver to organizations without making it feel like you will need to add a twenty-fifth hour in the day just to have a successful Twitter presence.

Before getting started on the automation task, it is imperative that you take the time to learn the positives and negatives of automation early in your social media strategy. Your social media strategy can only be successful if you think through each decision on what to automate and what to pass on. Automating for the sake of having something on your feed is not a good idea. It will not help strengthen your Twitter presence, and it can only hurt the image that you are trying to convey. The purpose of your Twitter feed (the idea of having a Twitter account in general) should not be for the sake of having one. If this is your main objective, it is probably best to delete your Twitter account and focus on using social media that works better for your organizational needs.

There are many positives for automating your feed, but there are negatives as well. Do not go blindly into automation. If you start the journey of automation without knowing what you are getting into, it will leave you with more work and stress than it is worth in the end. When you make the decision to automate your feed, you will also need to know when to stop automation if it is not working for your community.

The word "automation" has been mentioned a few times in this chapter, but it may not be clear what "automation" means exactly. Automation is the act of not manually doing something. You are using a tool to assist with your tasks. You can think of it as a washing machine for your Twitter account. Sure, you could hand wash your clothing, but it would take a lot of unnecessary time. Time is a luxury that most do not have in their busy schedule. This is why most use washing machines to have clean clothing to wear on a daily basis. It is a similar concept on why you should consider automation for your Twitter feed. You may be the sole person responsible for your feed. If you take the time to learn what can be automated, you could save a lot of time and effort to focus on bigger and better engagement strategies. There are guidelines about automation on Twitter. Be mindful as it can be considering spamming if done repeatedly and excessively. You can look at the Twitter guidelines (it is meant for developers, but it is a useful link when looking at automation): support.twitter.com/articles/76915.

AUTOMATION TOOLS

Before learning how you can automate certain tasks in Twitter, you need to research what type of tool will work best for your organization. Then you can begin the process of automation once you have properly researched your options. This is a rundown of the different management tools (free and paid) that can be used to help automate your feed's content and beyond. Hootsuite and TweetDeck were addressed in chapter 3, but these tools will be addressed again in the context of how they can help with automation. There are two other tools to discuss: Buffer and SocialOomph. This is not meant to be an exhaustive list. The highlighted tools are ones that in our research we found to be the most useful to include in this book.

A good blog article that has nine tools that can help with your automation needs can be found here: blog.thesocialms.com/9-twitter-automation-tools-save-time/. Some of the tools that are mentioned we have not researched properly, but feel free to explore these tools before making any decisions.

These tools will not only automate your tweets, but they can help manage your social networks. These tools will analyze your tweets, allow you to use RSS feeds to gather content, or even assist with social campaigns. It is important to look at each tool with a cohesive eye and not just choose a tool for one feature (for example, using the tool for scheduling daily tweets only). Do your own research, weigh the positives and negatives for each tool, and then decide which tool will work best for your organization's needs. Always remember to think about how well it will help you engage your community.

Hootsuite

In our research, we found that many organizations use Hootsuite (hootsuite.com) to manage their Twitter feeds (along with their other social media networks). Some may use the paid version of this management tool. The free version of Hootsuite features:

- the ability to manage three different social networks,
- the ability to schedule thirty posts per month,
- basic analytics, and
- two RSS feed integrations to find and share content.

In the different paid versions from Professional (starts at $19 USD per month) to Enterprise (which is customized for your organization), the ability to manage more social networks is available, as well as unlimited scheduling and RSS feed integrations. There is also real-time analytics and increased online support. Hootsuite provides a thirty-day free trial, so if you are having cold feet about investing in a product, your organization can try out the paid features before taking the plunge on this product. It should be noted that Hootsuite does not support automatic messages, replies, and follows options.

TweetDeck

TweetDeck (tweetdeck.twitter.com) is owned by Twitter. This is a free tool that will only help with your Twitter automation. At this point, there are no paid versions available that offer more than the free version. If you are looking for a management tool for several social media networks, TweetDeck is not for you. TweetDeck will only manage different Twitter accounts; it will not manage different social networks, like Facebook or Instagram. It will allow multiple users to manage the Twitter accounts. Be sure that when you log in, you are not confusing your personal and professional accounts if you manage both. TweetDeck features the following:

- allows scheduling tweets;
- allows the creation of Twitter collections, made by your organization; and

- provides a column view of the activity on Twitter for multiple Twitter accounts.

In short, TweetDeck serves those that only have a Twitter presence or do not mind the idea of using different tools for different social networks. If you just need a tool to schedule and view your tweets and to make sure you are keeping up to date with the activity happening in the @ mentions and the curated collections and lists of the Twitter accounts linked, TweetDeck will suit your needs. TweetDeck does not support automatic following, message, and replies. TweetDeck also does not have RSS integration or analytics. Twitter does support analytics though and can be used directly from the Twitter homepage. Analytics will be discussed in more depth in chapter 7.

Buffer

Buffer (buffer.com) is a management tool that allows you to schedule, analyze, and manage your social networks. Buffer mainly serves to post and analyze, while TweetDeck and Hootsuite will allow you to see your feed in action. You can interact and view other Twitter feeds, but with Buffer, this tool is strictly for scheduling tweets, analyzing how those tweets are performing, and discovering content to use in your scheduled tweets. The free version of Buffer features the following:

- three social media accounts only (In the free version, it supports Twitter, Facebook, Linked In, Google+, and Instagram. You can have three Twitter accounts connected or one of each social media platform, but it cannot exceed three accounts in the free version. In the paid version, it supports Pinterest as well and more connected accounts.);
- ten scheduled posts in your queue with no daily, monthly, or yearly limits;
- allows you to schedule as you browse with a free plug-in for browsers;
- a video and gif uploader; and
- link shortening only.

The free version of Buffer does not support RSS integration or analytics; in order to get those features, a paid version of Buffer will need to be purchased. There are different paid version levels, starting with Awesome ($10 per month, for increased scheduled posts [100]) and going up to the Enterprise version, which is catered to your organization. Buffer also gives seven-day trials for Awesome and fourteen-day trials for the Team and Enterprise versions. Trials are pretty effective and helpful to scope out exactly what interface works best for you and what features work best for you, without having to worry about spending unnecessary budget money.

SocialOomph

SocialOomph (www.socialoomph.com) is one of the tools that our research showed will support auto-follow and messages features. These are features to be really careful with when deciding how to implement your social media strategy. These features will be highlighted here as an option to give you the whole picture when looking for the correct automation tool for your organization. SocialOomph has free and professional versions, and it has additional features to be paid for separately. The free version includes the following:

- scheduled tweets,
- track keywords and replies,
- save and reuse drafts,
- URL shortening—to track your tweets,
- view mentions and retweets,
- purge your tweets and messages without losing your followers, and
- manage up to five Twitter accounts.

With the professional version of SocialOomph, you will be able to manage other social networks (Facebook, LinkedIn) and find quality followers on Twitter; for example, there are features to weed out spammers and sort your followers into customized lists, and for additional fees, SocialOomph will send you a list of your followers and the option to auto-follow these new followers. SocialOomph's professional version starts at $17.97 and is billed in a two-week cycle. The price can increase or decrease depending on what features you need.

AUTOMATING TASKS

After doing your proper research, you will make your decision on what tool (or tools) will work best for your organization's time and perhaps budget, if you decide to utilize paid features in your automation plan. There are several tasks that can be automated, and some will require additional setup and tools. These added tools and services may be something that your organization values and may be worth the extra time, effort, and possibly budget to enable the tool to be used. Here are the four different types of tasks that can be automated:

- Twitter direct messages,
- Twitter @replies,
- Twitter followers, and
- Twitter posts (which are your tweets).

When you are on Twitter, you can direct message your followers. If a follower is following you, it will appear in their inbox. If they are not following you, it will appear in the Requests box. You can choose to direct message automatically, for example, when they start following your Twitter feed. They will receive a direct message immediately after following your Twitter account. The positive of this strategy is that you can make direct contact with your community immediately. You can set up a standard message. Perhaps it can be a short message that will thank your new follower and give the follower a helpful hint about other services within your organization. But it can also be looked at negatively and come across as impersonal and/or robotic. This is a strategy to tread lightly with and requires thinking about your social media strategy's ultimate goal. Automating direct messages is a feature that isn't available in every tool mentioned above; it is a feature that you may have to set up using different tools. It is also something that Twitter does not condone, as it can be considered spamming your followers. As noted in a Sprout Social post: "Automatic Direct Messages in Twitter are often frowned upon because they make you look like you don't care about your followers. They sound like generic marketing messages that could be directed at anyone. There's no personalization and customers are savvy enough today to tell."

As Sprout Social will note, it does not mean that you should not use automated tools for Twitter: "In the end, we're big fans of batching your posts. Take a few hours each week to schedule out your posts in advance or to fill in gaps in the month. You'll worry less on if you posted today on Instagram and spend important time engaging with your community" (Chen 2017). Batching posts simply means that you are taking the time to schedule posts in advance; as stated you can take an hour or so and post a few posts to ensure that you have content, instead of rushing and wasting your time worrying if you posted at all on a given day and time. It is more valuable to engage with your community than to have a bunch of posts lined up that are not making any impact at all. This is an important tip to remember: engage and interact; do not post and dictate.

There are certain ways to build in automation by having ongoing services that will need consistent promotion; for example, many museums and archives have exhibits and giving these exhibits a push on your Twitter feed can develop great engagement over time. Looking at the Newseum presence (@newseum), their team is focused on their mission of the importance of a free press and First Amendment rights. Their feed curates what is on exhibit and what events are happening in the world. It is a blend of automated and manual that can be adapted for all organizations. It is really important to hone in on your mission as stated in the first chapter of this book.

When using automation tools, it is important to not be careless. You need to be careful and wary of how you utilize these tools as they may not perform the way you intended them to perform. If you are feeling overwhelmed or confused by having too many management tools, reconsider your options. Weigh the positives and negatives of automating a message to your followers; it may be best to reserve your time and energy on your Twitter feed, as this is where the engagement will foster and cultivate interaction within your community. A good example of using direct messages can be shown through a recent Springshare interaction. Springshare is the company responsible for powering Libguides (as well as a suite of other products) for the library community. There were two outages in a span of one month, which occurred at the beginning of the fall semester for many college and university libraries. This is a public relations nightmare. But Springshare utilized their Twitter presence by posting timely (and lighthearted) tweets about the situation at hand. They gained many followers from the untimely outage that took place, and they used the opportunity to make a direct message connection. When someone followed the account during the outage, this is the message that was received:

springshare
@springshare

Thanks for following us @springshare - apologies that the circumstances for your follow aren't ideal! But, silver lining, in addition to getting information about the recent outage you'll also get our Springy Tips & Tricks, cool sites and systems we highlight, and more!

Figure 5.1. Example of an effective use of automated direct messages on Twitter. *Springshare*

This is an example of using automation to cultivate interactions—and make it seem less robotic by capturing the follower in a time of need—and showing the worth of utilizing Twitter to gain the support and trust needed to have your organization succeed.

This strategy applies to Twitter replies and followers. It is generally frowned upon by most marketing experts to automatically follow or reply to content on your feeds. The Coca-Cola Twitter campaign will be described in detail later on in the chapter, but *AdWeek* was very direct about their distaste for automated marketing campaigns: "However, automating an entire marketing cam-

paign can result in embarrassment, ridicule and lost business. So learn from Coca-Cola and stay attentive during your next Twitter marketing campaign" (Dugan 2015).

There are different exceptions to this rule. To recap, the @ symbol in Twitter refers to the reply on a tweet; @ replies can be seen by everyone that follows you, as well as the intended account. So if you decide that your account will automatically send a tweet without looking at the content, that can be a disaster. It is not smart to automate any task that you do not have control over or have oversight on. We will address the idea of Twitter bots later on in this chapter and give examples on creative ways to use Twitter bots and how they can be a welcome addition to your social media strategy. But, briefly, Twitter bots are accounts created to automatically reply and interact with followers based on queries.

The one task that automation can definitely benefit is automating your posts. Here are several Twitter posts that can be automated to save you time and also keep you feed current:

- Evergreen posts that aren't time sensitive. Marketing experts have agreed that posting at 1 p.m. on weekdays in your time zone is the most popular time for engagement (Lee 2016). It could be a smart move to always have something scheduled for this time. Perhaps you can use this scheduled tweet to remind about a certain resource that you are trying to promote.
- Events or holiday closings posts. For example, if you have story time every week at a certain time, you can schedule reminder marketing tweet posts in advance.

John Jackson, head of outreach and communications at Loyola Marymount University (LMU) Libraries (@LMULibrary), described the process of utilizing Hootsuite Enterprise (which the library cost shares with other campus units) to schedule tweets throughout the week. In this sample snapshot of the Hootsuite Enterprise tool, please note the use of scheduling tweets at a similar time and the type of tweet that is being scheduled.

Figure 5.2.   Handling automation of Twitter posts on Hootsuite. *Loyola Marymount University Libraries*

By scheduling similar tweets at a similar time, this organization shows the value of having a good strategy set in place to ensure that their Twitter presence remains active: automating the posts for similar content that is considered evergreen, content that can sustain without timeliness as a factor. Jackson also described that more real-time and current tweets do not occur in their scheduled tweets as a way to make sure their feed is always current.

Studies show that greater engagement comes from participatory tweets and campaigns that get your community involved, rather than the broadcasting of events and doing public relations for your organization. One study in particular collected Twitter posts from forty-eight museums across the United States and evaluated how Twitter engages with visitors of these museums. While the study's results are not promising, it provides the details of why certain types of tweets are better than others when speaking of engagement strategies.

To a larger degree the activity observed by museums in the sample was focused on one-to-many traditional communication. Those activities require and elicit fewer (or lesser) participatory behavior from a museum's Twitter followers. Even posting "fact of the day" information to Twitter, an arguably less marketing-driven and more educationally driven activity does not prompt responses from visitors. By contrast, some museums in the study were in-

viting participation by taking a concept like "fact of the day" and turning it in a game where a picture of a collections item would be accompanied by asking Twitter followers to make a guess about the photo's content. Livetweeting an event also invited online visitors to join a conversation about a program happening at the museum. (Langa 2014)

It is important to mention that just automating your feed with content on a weekly basis is not enough to make a real impact on your engagement strategy. It is imperative to look at the kind of tweets and make sure they are landing with your community. This will be discussed in chapter 7. Making this a priority early on in your strategy will give your feed the personal touch that your community will notice. The best way is to use automation to help, not hinder, your presence. You will need a combination of both automated and manual tweets to make your Twitter feed really come to life.

TWITTER BOTS

Twitter bots have a mixed reputation. Some may say that it is a risky move to have Twitter bots because it is automated content that you may not have control over, and it can cause faux pas without your intent. In an original e-mail exchange with Mary Claire Morris, communications and marketing manager

Figure 5.3.   A Twitter bot in action. *New York Public Library*

at University of Michigan (U-M) Libraries (@ UMichLibrary), she reported that a library bot had been created and implemented, but in a later e-mail exchange, there had been a change: "Well, there is an update about the bot. U-M's central director of social media has decreed there shall be no bots! We've killed it. I do understand her concern, since a bot that automatically shoots out content without taking into account breaking news could inadvertently tweet something controversial or insensitive."

Creating a Twitter bot adds another level of caution, but if you can monitor and engage properly, it can be a great engagement tool. A good example of this is the New York Public Library's Emoji Bot (@ NYPLEmoji)—this bot has clearly defined information right in its Twitter bio and does a cool job of showcasing the digital collections of the New York Public Library via the prompt of emojis.

With Twitter bots or automated hashtag campaigns, you have to be wary of other people's intentions when embarking on these types of campaigns; some of the world's biggest companies have had bad experiences when dealing with automation. Digiday .com reported on the biggest failures with automated campaigns: "Coca-Cola suspended its Super Bowl-timed, automated social campaign #MakeItHappy, when Gawker tricked the brand into tweeting out a number of lines from Adolf Hitler's *Mein Kampf.* In the campaign, Coke asked people to respond to negative tweets with positive ones—using an ASCII code to convert their tweets into images like singing cats and sunglass-wearing palm trees" (Dua 2014).

Sometimes even the most well-intended Twitter campaign can fail because of a lack of human touch. With all automated tasks, it is important to manage them; you cannot just set it and forget it like the old infomercials for Ronco rotisserie ovens. This will only cause your Twitter strategy to implode before your very eyes before it even begins.

It is of great interest to look at how certain museums have used chatbots to gamify the visiting experience at their organizations. "The Cooper-Hewitt Museum in New York has undoubtedly been a pioneer in chatbot technologies. As early as 2013 they created Object Phone—a service powered by Twillio that you could text or call to ask for more information on a museum object" (Ashri 2017). This article mentions how certain museums have had success with chatbots, and these types of interactions can be easily adapted to a Twitter bot with the right technology and energy. Many organizations can benefit from attempting to utilize this type of strategy. There are a variety of ways to enable bots to work with your needs, but make sure you are ready to embark on the journey before you delve into the automation of creating a bot. It is important to have defined parameters for your bot and not to just half-think the idea. And, if you do not feel like it is working, it is OK to pull the plug. It is better to try and fail than to keep a failing Twitter presence, like a bot, in action, without updating or engaging with your community.

There are also ways to monitor bots and promote them to your community as a value-added bonus. Maybe you do not have the know-how or the time to invest in creating a bot, but you want to make sure that your community is aware of how bots work; or maybe as the Twitter administrator, you need to know how many of your followers are real. Here are a few tools to help with tracking and monitoring bots:

- TwitterAudit (www.twitteraudit.com/)—the first audit is free; you simply enter your Twitter handle. If you want more audits, it will cost you a fee.
- Botcheck.me (botcheck.me/)—this will detect and track political propaganda.

CROSS-PLATFORM PUBLISHING

To end this chapter, let's delve into cross-platform publishing. Automation of your Twitter presence can be tricky, and then you will have to add in the idea of cross-platform publishing. It can be something that becomes a little unwieldy if you do not have the right social media strategy in mind and if you are not in tune with your community. Looking at your community's needs and surveying what works best on different social networks make the difference.

Kaitlyn Vella, social media manager at MTV Networks (@MTV), described MTV's strategy with cross-platform publishing:

> The Facebook audience is much different than the Twitter audience. Where a user on Facebook might want to just read an article or watch a video and move onto the next, a Twitter user is generally looking to have more of a conversation. If we share on article on Twitter, the chances of it getting a ton of clicks isn't that high. Instead of clickthroughs, though, we're seeing more people retweeting and liking the article. We also found that talking like our audience on Twitter is what works best, at least in the sense of MTV. Our audience (of generally 13-30-year olds) doesn't want to be talked at or talked down to. They're smart, they have opinions, and they want to be involved in the conversation.

Being mindful of your community's needs definitely will help with your engagement. As noted in chapter 1, the social media strategy is crucial to your community engagement success. Take a page from MTV's strategy of knowing their audience and speaking directly to them and not at them. The idea that you are listening to your community and not just talking at them is a very important part of cultivating relationships. In our research, we found a report about the five steps to effective engagement:

- Target your outreach.
- Invite valuable contributions.
- Cultivate productive interaction.
- Honor community work.
- Learn and improve.

Taking the time to really dissect that third step, which is to cultivate productive interaction, is what automation of your feed is about. Guzmán states: "But if you want your engagement to have its maximum effect, there are two important things you can do to fuel it. You can reach out directly to people who draw the strongest contributions, and

you can participate in the discussion or exchange of material yourself" (Guzmán 2016). It is about taking the time to understand what you can handle on your own, in real time, and what you can depend on a tool to do to help showcase your content. This is how you cultivate those relationships with your Twitter presence. Look at what you can do yourself and then look at how you can collaborate to enrich the experience for all involved.

More on Cross-Platform Publishing

You will notice that certain social media platforms do not work together as nicely as you would like. Here is an example of this: Instagram has chosen to block photos from automatically appearing within a tweet. There is a workaround for this, according to a handy Medium article: "Many people are using services such as IFTTT and Zapier to tweet their Instagram photos using the Twitter API" (Köhlbrugge 2017). You will need to sign up for a Zapier or IFTTT account. IFTTT is a free way to get all of your apps and platforms to work together. You can sign up at ifttt.com. Zapier is another automation tool that helps make your Internet world a little easier; you can sign up at zapier.com.

In the next chapter, we will discuss how push publishing can further enhance engagement and build up the idea of seizing the opportunity to get your community involved in your social media presence. Automation is just a starting point to utilizing tools to enable your feed to reach and interact with your community, while allowing you the opportunity to hone in on other areas of your strategy.

REFERENCES

Ashri, Ronald. "How Museums are Using ChatBots." *Chatbots*. 2017. chatbotsmagazine.com/how-museums-are-using-chatbots-5-real-world-examples-34e9d4858dd9.

Chen, J. "Social Media Automated Rules No Brand Should Break." Sprout Social. 2017. sproutsocial.com/insights/social-media-automation/.

Dua, T. "5 Biggest Bot Fails by Brands on Twitter." *Digiday*. 2014. digiday.com/marketing/5-biggest-bot-fails-brands-twitter/.

Dugan, L. "Why You Should Never Automate Your Twitter Marketing Campaigns." *AdWeek*. 2015. www.adweek.com/digital/automate-twitter-marketing/.

Guzmán, M. "How to Engage Your Audience in 5 Key Steps." American Press Institute. 2016. www.americanpressinstitute.org/publications/reports/strategy-studies/5-steps-engagement/.

Köhlbrugge, M. "A Better Way to Post Your Instagram Photos to Twitter." Medium. 2017. medium.com/@marckohlbrugge/a-better-way-to-post-your-instagram-photos-to-twitter-7f3a04a37d89.

Langa, L. A. "Does Twitter Help Museums Engage with Visitors?" iConference 2014 Proceedings, March 4–7, 2014, Berlin, 484–495.

Lee, K. "The Biggest Social Media Study: What 4.8 Million Tweets Say about the Best Time to Tweet." Buffer. 2016. blog.bufferapp.com/best-time-to-tweet-research.

6

Push Publishing

At this point, we have discussed how to bring your Twitter presence to life. All of the chapters before this have brought you here, and in chapter 5, we discussed the concept of pull publishing. Now we will introduce the concept of push publishing. You might be thinking, what is pull vs. push publishing, what is the difference, and what does this have to do with my Twitter feed? Looking at *PC Magazine* for guidance on what pull and push technologies are, these definitions should help clarify and bring an understanding to what these concepts mean for Twitter publishing. Pull technology is as follows: "Specifically requesting information from a particular source. Downloading Web pages via a Web browser is an example of pull technology. Getting mail is also pull technology if the user initiates a request to retrieve it." As we discussed in the previous chapter, this is the act of getting content from other sources. With this chapter on push publishing, we will discuss how to push content away from Twitter to different sources. Push technology is as follows:

> Transmitting data from an internal network or a cloud-based service to the user's computer or mobile device. Notifications for a wide variety of events as well as stock quotes and text messages are pushed in real time. In contrast, e-mail and various types of updates are typically pushed at intervals. Cloud-based services push people's personal photos, videos and documents to all their devices to keep them in sync. Automatic updates

to applications are also a form of push technology. (*PC Magazine* n.d.)

Well, now that you have created a Twitter feed for your organization, how will people discover it? It is the age-old question: if you build it, will they come? The answer lies in your push publishing strategies.

Again to recap the pull vs. push publishing concept, pulling content from other sources, such as an RSS feed or from a source outside of Twitter, is pull publishing. It is the act of pulling or taking content from somewhere else and putting it into your feed. We spent time discussing pull publishing and automation in chapter 5. Now we will discuss push publishing. When you push content, you are creating a poster or billboard for your organization by pushing your Twitter outside of the Twittersphere and having it live on your website or another platform that is not Twitter. There are different ways to do this, and it takes a little technology know-how, but there are plenty of tutorials on the web to help guide you.

The question of push publishing deals with your marketing plan and how people will find your Twitter feed. We discussed this in chapter 2, but this is more about how to market your Twitter feed and make it even more discoverable. Sure, people can find your Twitter feed directly on Twitter, but this is not a sure-fire approach. Some research has shown that collaboration within your organization can strengthen your presence as well.

A study performed regarding social media strategy at the Albertsons Library at Boise State University noted:

> The Marketing Minds group at Boise State is comprised of social media managers from all over campus. The social media team at Albertsons Library presented at a Marketing Minds meeting on new tools being utilized and how we were sharing them. In addition, the social media team at Albertsons Library participated in an email group that sends out calls and requests for shared promotions; we share information relevant to our students on our social networks, such as Financial Aid due dates, important information from the student government group Associated Students of Boise State University (ASBSU), and pertinent events. (Ramsey and Vecchione 2014)

Having a collaborative effort between departments at a university helps the community as a whole to receive the value-added content. This can relate to other organizations, such as archives and museums. This may not be possible at a small organization, but collaboration is a key in building your Twitter presence. Perhaps it can be as simple as making connections within your community's reach. If you are the sole person at the hospital library, you can reach out to doctors and nurses to boost your Twitter presence. Talk to them and ask them what kind of information they would like to see; it is imperative that you listen to your intended audience. You want to increase that potential, and you can increase that potential by making sure your community is aware of your presence and is engaging on there as well. Use the opportunity to make the right people at your organization aware of what you have to offer. You have spent a lot of time and energy on building up your feed, and what will be the point if no one knows that it even exists? This is why planning to highlight your Twitter (and social media in general) on your organization's website and building it into your brand can be a crucial step for achieving maximum success.

EMBEDDING TWEETS

What does it mean to embed something? Well, luckily, Twitter has made it easier to define exactly what it means to embed or push your tweets outside of Twitter. You can check out how to do so by looking at the following support link: support.twitter.com/articles/20170071. Looking at this link, you will notice that even Twitter breaks down how much of your Twitter feed you may want to push (or embed as it is referred to) outside of the Twittersphere. Let's take the time to review different ways to push out your feed beyond the Twittersphere:

- single tweet
- stream of tweets
- Twitter lists or favorites
- timeline (which is a collection of your feed)
- Twitter search
- linking out/buttons

We will consider six different ways to embed your Twitter presence into your website and other platforms through the concept of push publishing. You can make the call on what is right for your organization. Do you want to share your feed on your website or with a simple button? This is a part of your social media strategy, and how people discover your feed can be something that you track in your analytics (more on that in the next chapter) to see exactly what works best for your organization in the long run.

Embedding a single tweet is a simple way to start the process of making your audience aware of your Twitter presence. You can simply embed a single tweet on Facebook. It can be effective if you are trying to direct non-followers to important conversations occurring on Twitter. For example, if you can direct your audience to follow you on Twitter, this is usually a good way to build engagement. If you have a great presence on Facebook but a lackluster following on Twitter, you can decide to showcase a tweet that will entice your audience to join your Twitter presence.

Another strategy for single tweet embedding is to run a contest or promotion on Twitter. Your organization can be successful using Twitter to get followers and engage your audience to get involved. Giving your community the chance to use their creativity or doing a fun giveaway can be the right incentive to get your audience to follow your Twitter feed. You do not have to give away a huge prize or make incredible promises in order for this to work. It could be a simple contest to help highlight an author visit. You could host a Twitter giveaway to win a signed copy of the author's book. Make sure that you have clearance and rights to do giveaways or promotions at your organization. If you aren't able to do that, you can run contests to highlight creativity. Every April, there is a National Library Week, and many libraries participate in "best shelfie" contests; it is a great way to get your community involved by having them take photos of their bookshelves and having the brag prize of being best. With a little creativity, you can run contests like this to cater to your community. Sprout Social shares some tips on how to launch a successful promotion on Twitter: "Twitter's conversational nature makes it ideal for brands that want to build relationships with their audience rather than just broadcast their message." This tip coupled with the key ingredients listed below can be the recipe for success for a Twitter promotion:

- Know your audience.
- Set your goal.
- Timing.
- Strategize.
- Provide value. (Jackson 2017)

Being successful with your Twitter promotion will take some research, but it is worth it to know what you are getting involved in and not to go into it blindly.

Here are a few more examples of promotions:

- Fun trivia contests: test your community's knowledge on a local city, museum, or particular subject. There are endless possibilities with trivia scenarios.
- Ask your community how they use your organization; use the opportunity to get the community talking about your resources.
- Highlight special talents by having them create works of arts or use their creative writing skills.

The archives community has a successful campaign on Twitter, and it happens on Valentine's Day. The hashtag #ArchivesValentines is used to share creative spins on the archival and records management lingo; it helps to engage the community in what these professionals are doing with a fun twist. In a phone conversation with the Utah Division of Archives and

Figure 6.1. Examples from the #ArchivesValentines campaign. *Utah Division of Archives and Records Services*

Figure 6.2. Examples from the #ArchivesValentines campaign. *United States National Archives*

Records Service (@recordkeepers), the #ArchivesValentines campaign was mentioned and how far the reach of such a campaign went. They received additional followers and retweets from Europe. Their only concern was how to keep the engagement with these followers after the campaign was over. This is an important aspect to note, especially when embarking on engagement campaigns based on promotions or holiday themes. It is smart to think about how your feed will be for those who may find your Twitter from these types of campaigns and to ensure that you still have content on your Twitter page that they will find useful.

Single tweets are one way of drawing in followers; you can also embed a stream of tweets from a conversation to further emphasize that engagement is happening. If you find that you are having a great discussion on Twitter, make it known. This is where you can use marketing to really get your followers to take notice. If your followers are pleased, they will let others know and it will spread the positive image for your organization as a whole, not just on Twitter. Both approaches are pretty simple to do and are done to emphasize a key tweet or interaction, rather than the whole timeline. If you embed a tweet, this may be a good engagement tool to make those who are not following join and follow the conversation. With that said, it is important to note that your tweets must be public as you are not able to embed private tweets.

But if you are looking to have a more lasting presence, embedding a timeline right into your website will showcase exactly what is happening on Twitter. This is why it is very important to make sure your feed is current and active. If you tweet something, and people start responding and interacting, and you aren't there—it could be a flop for your engagement strategy. You can go to publish

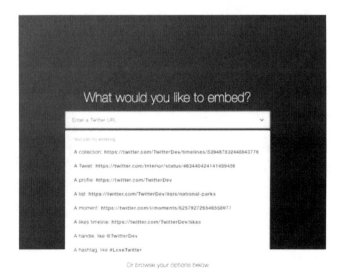

Figure 6.3.   Twitter publishing tool in action. *Twitter*

.twitter.com and simply choose what you want to embed, and it will give you the code. Minimal coding experience is required, which is great for those who are a little shy about delving into Twitter because they do not feel tech savvy enough. Figure 6.3 shows how easy it really is.

The Twitter publishing tool makes it very easy to push the code into your website. But sometimes it is not as easy as simply giving the code to your web team. Embedding a timeline into your website will take a little buy-in from your organization's web team as they may have their own ideas and visions for the look and feel of the website. Embedding Twitter may not be a priority or a part of the vision for them, and it is important to discuss this with your organization's web team before moving forward with a strategy that is centered on it. Some libraries have this built-in or envisioned when they redesign a website for their libraries, and other libraries may not have any say on how the website is constructed. In an e-mail interview, John Jackson, head of outreach and communications at Loyola Marymount University (LMU) Libraries (@LMU-Library), discussed the importance that LMU felt about embedding their Twitter feed on their library homepage: "We intentionally chose to create a space for our live Twitter feed on our homepage when our site was redesigned last year. This is the easiest way to push out 'service announcements' and to keep the content of the homepage fresh."

While it would help to have the possibility of having a Twitter feed embedded directly on your website, it may not be a possibility. It is easy to create the proper code due to Twitter's simple coding tools, but it may not happen due to your organization's technical staff, vision, and other various factors that you may not have control over, and it is nothing to worry about too much. Do not get discouraged or feel defeated if you are not able to get your feed directly embedded on the website. There are other creative ways to use embed tools to get your engagement up and running. If embedding a timeline is not a possibility, you can ask for space on the website for social media buttons that will push out to the feed. Most WordPress pages will have built-in plug-ins to showcase social media buttons; if your organization uses any kind of content management system (CMS), it will have the capability to integrate buttons to market your various social

Figure 6.4.　Example of an embedded Twitter feed on a library homepage. *Loyola Marymount University Libraries*

media icons, which includes Twitter. Many organizations have footers or headers with "Follow Us" or "Stay Connected" on their website in order to direct the community to their social media presence. This can work for your community's needs and will make your presence known. Do not forget about obvious oversight at times: you can add your Twitter handle to your e-mail signature or you can embed the last tweet in your signature. You may interact with many people via e-mail exchanges, so marketing your Twitter on that platform is a wise decision to boost visibility.

You can also use e-mail for marketing purposes. If your organization has a newsletter or it does an e-mail blast for important announcements, you can use this to embed a single tweet to promote a contest or to simply notify that you have a Twitter presence. If you want a more lasting effect, build engagement and use the opportunity to highlight why your community should follow you. Ultimately, it is a matter of convincing your community that Twitter is an asset, and this is the ultimate goal of engagement. You want your community to keep coming back after that initial follow or click to see what your Twitter feed is all about in the end.

CREATING AND EMBEDDING CUSTOM FEEDS

Looking at your community's needs and thinking about how to really cultivate productive interac-

tion is a concept that was discussed in chapter 5. Embedding tweets by utilizing hashtags and custom searches really narrows in and crafts your engagement strategy.

While you can choose to embed your Twitter feed entirely, there are custom feeds that may work better for your community's needs. A custom feed is a collection of tweets based on a hashtag or a custom search. We discussed this in depth in chapter 4, but, as a short recap, you have the ability to create hashtags and custom searches for your community. You can make a hashtag for a live event, tweet about it, and put this feed right on your website so those who are not present can follow along; this is a great engagement strategy to get your community involved in events that they may not be able to attend. In an interview, Ellen Lai, social media manager at Craig Newmark Graduate School of Journalism at City University of New York (CUNY), explained her strategies of introducing custom hashtags for live events. For example, she notes that she will alert the community before said event that there will be a hashtag to use for the live event and then promote it to ensure that the hashtag gains the proper amount of visibility before the actual live event takes place. This is done to get maximum exposure and to hopefully trend on Twitter. When your hashtag trends locally, it is a surefire way of knowing that you have a captive audience discussing what you are promoting as an organization. There are various ways to make sure that your community is well aware of the hashtags that your organization may use for live events or just on a continuous basis: you can send an e-mail blast or cross-promote on a different social media platform as well. This type of live tweeting and participatory tweeting has a greater return on engagement.

You can also make custom searches based on a hot topic in your community. By creating timely custom searches, it shows that you are in tune with your community's needs. If you are a high school librarian and your community is preparing for college entrance exams, this is a good time to flex your research muscles and create feeds. If you create a feed that helps them understand and get vital information about these exams, you are showing then the value of engaging on Twitter.

These are the different ways to use hashtags and custom searches, but you can take it to the next level by embedding these hashtags or custom searches directly on your website or even doing an e-mail blast to encourage participation, if website space is not in the cards. By creating a custom space via a hashtag, you are giving your community the ability to create a niche spot for their needs. This is an ongoing practice, and you can make great strides in creating a community. A great example in the library world is the hashtag community surrounding #critlib. There are weekly chats but also a continual presence on Twitter to discuss the issues that occur in the field of critical librarianship. This hashtag has been successful enough to warrant an in-person symposium—if you are interested, please do research the Critical Librarianship and Pedagogy Symposium (CLAPS). A recent Twitter post notes that a second symposium is in the works for 2018 (via @nope4evr). This has created a lot of research and awards for certain librarians. This is a very important example of how a hashtag on a particular topic can spread its wings beyond the Twitter world to really fulfill the potential engagement strategy.

In addition to custom searches and hashtags, you can create custom lists. A custom list is a curated list of Twitter users based on a particular topic or subject. Twitter has a very helpful support site for all the buzzwords used on Twitter and how to set up lists and such; you can check out the one on Twitter lists here: support.twitter.com/articles/76460. As an example, you are responsible for a small art library at your university, and you decide that you want to keep track of all of the museums in your community. You

can create a list of all the museums in your community; you can make connections with those museums as well. Then you can push out this list to your followers and they will have this valuable information at their fingertips. This strategy grew in popularity for many journalists, in particular, as it is a way to keep up with their reporting beats (a beat is a commonly used phrase in journalism to describe a journalist's niche or specialty area that they are reporting on; for example, the crime beat would be for those who cover crime stories). Poynter was one of many outlets that first created how-to guides on building Twitter lists to deepen reporting skills. To stress the importance, this quote embodies the power of curating Twitter lists effectively: "People on Twitter often ask me if I have three heads and six hands. No, I tell them, I have Twitter Lists" (Diamond 2012).

Taking a look at these tips will help your community; it is the way to get in touch with what is going on. Looking at the lists of your followers and even subscribing to a list will show engagement and get the notice of your followers, or non-followers for the same reason. Yes, there is a cool feature on Twitter that will allow you to subscribe to a list or be added to a list. It is a really great way to get your followers' engagement levels up. For example, if you work at an academic library, and you are the English subject specialist, you could make a list of all of the faculty members that teach English at your university; or if you are working at a public library, you can make a list of your local authors or key leaders in the community. Providing these types of lists can be considered service oriented and your community will appreciate that this is available. These types of lists can be done for archives, libraries, and museums alike. Look at what your community needs, and bring that information to them. You can push these lists out during key times and purposes. For example, if it is February and you want to highlight Black History Month, you can create a list of authors in your community who are African American. This concept can apply to many different types of curating, and the possibilities are endless when dealing with custom lists and searches. These lists and searches will not only help your organization, but it will develop a collaborative effort within your community. This will make them aware of your Twitter presence, but it will make them feel included in your strategy to get the community involved. Just be mindful when using custom lists and searches that you are not using someone else's curated content already, as you will not have the intended result you desire. Be aware of spelling of hashtags and properly research your lists to make sure you are not spreading fraudulent information. A little information literacy will make the difference for a negative impact versus a positive impact. According to the Association for College and Research Libraries (ACRL), information literacy is defined as "the set of integrated abilities encompassing the reflective discovery of information, the understanding of how information is produced and valued, and the use of information in creating new knowledge and participating ethically in communities of learning" ("Framework for Information Literacy" 2015).

This is crucial for your success as you evaluate the content that will be posted and disseminated to your community. If you are not able to evaluate and effectively select viable content to reach your community, your Twitter feed and your brand as a whole will suffer immensely. It should also be noted to look at respective guidelines in your organization's area of expertise. The fundamentals of information literacy may be the same across the board, but the context may differ and it is a good idea to be equipped with as much knowledge as possible. It is important to be engaged with your community's direct needs. Just because it works for one type of organization does not mean it will work for all. The concepts discussed throughout this book should be adaptable for many types of organizations. If you are reading this book, please keep in mind there is no one-size-fits-all strategy and you will need to adapt to your community and organization. With that said, here are some suggested links to look at for specific organizations:

- ALA Divisions: www.ala.org/aboutala/divs
- Art Libraries of North America: www.arlisna.org
- Association of Tribal Archives, Libraries, and Museums (ATALM): http://www.atalm.org
- Listing of Current Affiliates for American Library Association (ALA): http://www.ala.org/aboutala/affiliates/current
- Medical Library Association: www.mlanet.org
- Special Library Association: www.sla.org

- Society of American Archivists: www2.archivists.org
- American Alliance for Museums: www.aam-us.org
- ALA/SAA/AAM Committee on Archives, Libraries, and Museums (CALM): www.ala.org/aboutala/committees/joint/jnt-saa_ala

When you curate lists, searches, and hashtags, you are doing so with the ultimate goal of reaching out to your community and bringing them something that is not available elsewhere. You are giving them a glimpse into resources, giving them a voice to speak about something, giving them the opportunity to showcase their hidden or not so hidden talents—whatever it is, your Twitter engagement strategy should highlight your community and how you serve them.

In an e-mail interview, Dashka A. Gabriel, assistant manager of digital engagement for the Rubin Museum of Art (@RubinMuseum), explained their strategy for embedding Twitter: "We do embed tweets and other posts on our exhibition landing pages. These tweets are captured using the respective exhibition hashtag."

The OM LAB exhibition was a great example of positive engagement. It was an interactive exhibit where people could record their sounds. Their reactions and comments were captured on their website using the hashtag #OMLAB; when you visited the exhibition page, you had the option to tweet, and those tweets are pushing directly to the page as well:

Figure 6.5. Dedicated museum exhibition web page to encourage Twitter engagement. *Rubin Museum of Art*

The Rubin Museum has this type of strategy with most of their exhibitions, which is a great way to involve the community. It draws them right into the exhibition and utilizes the sounds for future exhibitions, but it also gives the community the opportunity to make comments and tweets directly at that moment.

Whether it is a hashtag, custom search, list, or even the tweets that your organization has marked as favorites, when you take the time to curate content for your community, and then push it into their inbox, their Facebook feed, or even just on the website, you are helping to engage your community and get them involved. Thinking about how to utilize pull and push publishing strategies, like the ones discussed in chapter 5 and this chapter, you can learn how to really make sure your community is served by how you deliver the content to them. Discovering the right blend of both strategies will help you tap into the community's heartbeat for what they need to remain engaged. Next, we will discuss how to measure your analytics. After all of your strategizing, it is time to decide if your strategy is working best for your community by tracking and measuring how well they interact with your organization's Twitter presence.

REFERENCES

Diamond, N. "8 Tips for Using Twitter Lists." Poynter Institute. 2012. www.poynter.org/news/8-tips-using-twitter-lists.

"Framework for Information Literacy for Higher Education." American Library Association. February 9, 2015. www.ala.org/acrl/standards/ilframework.

Jackson, D. "7 Tips to Launch a Successful Twitter Promotion." Sprout Social. 2017. sproutsocial.com/insights/twitter-promotions/.

Pagowsky, N. (nope4evr). "It's not 100% completely official yet (maybe at 98%?), but since a few people have asked: yes, we are planning another Critical Librarianship & Pedagogy Symposium (CLAPS) for this year—most likely November here in Tucson ✳ #critlib." Tweet. January 22, 2018, 11:25 a.m.

"Pull and Push Technology." *PC Magazine.* n.d. www.pcmag.com/encyclopedia/term/49977/push-technology.

Ramsey, E., and A. Vecchione. "Engaging Library Users through a Social Media Strategy." *Library Innovation* 5, no. 2 (2014): 71–82.

7

Using Analytics

In this final chapter, we will discuss how to analyze your engagement on Twitter. The previous chapters have helped you to create a successful engagement strategy on Twitter. We have equipped you with tips and tools on how to execute based on best practices and successful campaigns at different organizations. It is important to not just rely on best practice and what works for others; you will need to look at what works best for your organization. Analyzing your Twitter presence will make the difference in knowing if you are communicating effectively with your community.

What does it mean to analyze exactly? When we use the word "analyze" or to track, it is the process of looking at your Twitter presence and seeing how well your tweets are performing. Are your tweets excelling? Are they landing and reaching the followers you intended? Analyzing your Twitter feed will give you the data that you may need to support your endeavor to administration. Before we delve deeper, remember that you should become an expert in knowing the language and lingo of Twitter in order for your Twitter presence to succeed. Knowing the difference between a post (tweet) and a direct message (DM) can make a big difference in your strategy. When we run reports and analyze Twitter data, it is imperative to understand what we are looking at and what we are focusing on in order for the analytics to make sense and actually work for the betterment of your engagement strategy.

Let's briefly discuss how different tools will provide different access to analytics. If you decided to use TweetDeck for your software choice, you will need to select a different tool to measure analytics, as TweetDeck is solely a publishing platform. Many use Twitter's built-in analytic tool, as it is free and easy to manage. If you decided to use Hootsuite, there are select basic analytics for each tool that are included in the free version. If you decided to use Buffer for your needs, you will need to purchase a professional account to get analytics. Buffer will give you reach and posts, retweets, and recent tweets for certain periods of time. Hootsuite does provide basic analytics for free with free accounts, but it is not as comprehensive as some may want or need for engagement strategy performance data. With this said, if you want to use a different tool to measure your analytics, you can decide to utilize a free tool for your needs. Some may find it troublesome to remember different logins and passwords and maintain two management tools, but others may like the option of using free analytic tools to delve deeper into data to enhance their engagement strategies. Whatever you decide, use your own judgment on how to best serve your organization's needs. You can review and/or re-read chapters 3 and 5 for more in-depth discussions and tips on what tool to use to get started on Twitter and how it will relate to your analytics strategy. Right now, we will delve into introducing new tools that are dedicated solely to Twitter analytics.

DEDICATED TWITTER ANALYTICS TOOLS

We will discuss two new tools that may be of interest and can be beneficial to getting the most out of your Twitter engagement strategy. These two tools target how your Twitter presence is engaging and interacting with your community. These tools are free to use and do not require added budgetary costs. Each tool may have a special focus, such as reach, which is how far your tweets are going and who they are interacting with on a determined basis that you may choose. One of the major principles that this book promotes is to reach your community in ways that they want and need to be reached. Let's take a look at each of these tools to see what may work with your organization.

While we are highlighting two new tools, there are several out there; a simple Google search will turn up hundreds of results, but it is best to research before using any tool for Twitter. Brandwatch recommends ten free Twitter analysis tools that may be worthwhile: www.brandwatch.com/blog/top-10-free-twitter-analysis-tools/. The next two tools we will discuss appeared on the Brandwatch link.

TweetStats

TweetStats (www.tweetstats.com) is a tool that will measure your usage and timing. It is simple to use: you can just enter your twitter handle (i.e., @twittername), and it will give you your results on the web browser that you choose. It will work on mobile phones as well if you are interested in receiv-

ing stats on the go. If you are looking to keep track of your tweets on an hourly, daily, or weekly basis, you can use this tool to see how well your tweets are performing and how far they are traveling in comparison to other Twitter accounts. If you want to know how many posts your organization makes and how many times a day you are tweeting compared to another library in your city, you can use TweetStats to measure this. TweetStats provides these reports in a bar graph, and they are clickable to search within different time periods for particular usage points. This tool will also track your reply statistics, which is extremely helpful for engagement purposes. Seeing if your tweets actually get your followers replying and developing an exchange is crucial.

Tweet Reach

With Tweet Reach (www.tweetreach.com), you will need to create a Union Metrics account before you can obtain your free analytics. Like TweetStats, it is available to use on mobile devices for stats on the go. It is simple to create an account with an e-mail address and password. You will receive a welcome e-mail from Union Metrics shortly after, and you can begin crunching those data statistics within seconds. The free account includes unlimited snapshot reports for up to one hundred tweets posted in the past few days. If you require more or older tweets, Tweet Reach can do this for you for a fee. Like Hootsuite or Buffer, you can subscribe to their monthly business plans for more in-depth statistical analysis. But for those just starting out and with limited budgetary resources, you can use Tweet Reach for free to get enough data to see if you are on the right track with your engagement strategy. This is the major purpose of tracking your tweets and using analytic tools. With Tweet Reach, you can track anything from a hashtag (#hashtag) to a Twitter handle (@twitterhandle) or a set of keywords. This tool allows for reports to be done in seconds, which is pretty efficient for those multitasking. It will measure potential reach, impressions, and conversations. An added bonus is the ability to track a theme or campaign; for example, if you are interested in seeing how well a Twitter campaign for promoting a book event went, Tweet Reach will give you the

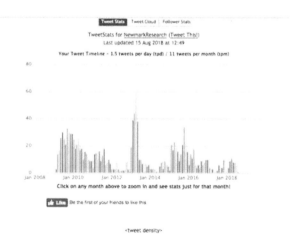

Figure 7.1.   TweetStats in action.

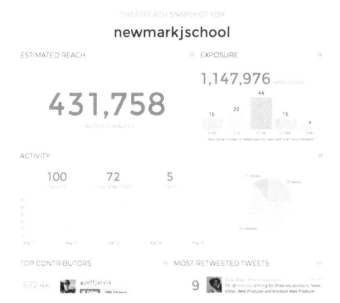

Figure 7.2. **Tweet Reach in action.**

stats on how well it performed and when it had the biggest impact. Tweet Reach will also analyze your posts from Instagram for the past month.

The next and last tool, Twitter Analytics, also appears on the Brandwatch link, but it is not a new tool per se, as we have discussed this tool in previous chapters.

Twitter Analytics

Last but certainly not least is Twitter's built-in analytic tool—it is free and it is quite comprehensive. Twitter Analytics (analytics.twitter.com) is free for anyone with a Twitter account. Twitter Analytics cannot be done via the mobile app, but you can use the web address for your mobile browser to get access on the go. From the account home page, you will see a variety of different metrics. The summary runs across the top of the page and breaks down into the following:

- Tweets
- Tweet Impressions
- Profile Visits
- Mentions
- Followers

All of this data is clickable and measurable with change graphs, showing growth or decline percentages from the previous periods (Twitter by default

measures twenty-eight-day periods). You can tweak this for your needs and see where you need to improve for future goals and objectives.

The home screen also includes tweet highlights:

- Top Tweet
- Top Mention
- Top Follower
- Top Media Tweet (a tweet that includes a video, photo, etc.)

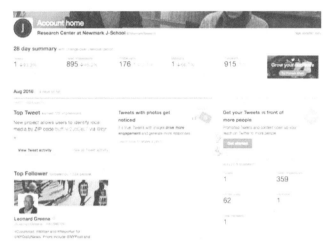

Figure 7.3 . **Twitter Analytics in action.**

It will also give the option to open and explore more in-depth activity by going to the followers dashboard or to see more tweet activity. If you decide to go beyond the home page, which is recommended, you will see the following tabs:

Tweets

In this tab, you will be able to measure and track how your tweets are performing. You can look at your Twitter activity, and Twitter will give you the impressions (how many times people looked at or saw your tweets) and the amount of engagements it received (replies and the retweets) and give you an engagement rate. This is all crucial for engagement purposes and seeing how well your tweets perform. You can see how many clicks you receive or how many retweets you are receiving all from this Tweets tab. You can see if it is the tone or the content that needs tweaking, or maybe it is the time of the day. This will all help you to engage with your followers better.

Audiences

In this tab, you will be able to measure and track how many followers you have or you lost in a specific period. It also provides insight into the type of followers you have and what they are tweeting about, or what they find important or valuable. This is also essential in terms of comparison; you can compare your followers to those that you follow to see if there are any gaps and how interests and demographics match. It is a powerful way to look at how your audience shapes up on Twitter; it will give you concrete interests and styles to know how your audience consumes information, even by gender, household income, and wireless carrier. It may seem like an overload of information, but it could prove to be an asset in terms of your engagement strategy. For example, if you notice that the majority of your followers have a particular interest in board games, it may be a program that your organization could consider for an event or purchasing materials. This is just one simple way to generate engagement strategies based on this audience data tracking.

Events

The Events tab shows various events happening on Twitter, for example, Valentine's Day or the Super Bowl. If you click on it to see how it is performing, it can give you some insights on how many tweets are being discussed about a particular event. It will give you the top tweets and the live tweets happening. This could be a beneficial tool to use for a live event at your organization when you want to capture how tweets are performing. It will also give you the option to create a new campaign if your budget allows—you can create campaigns for new followers, tweet engagements, promoted videos, and more—if you feel that this is something that you want to invest in. You can always attempt to do more grassroots and do-it-yourself campaigns to get your Twitter presence going. We discussed these campaigns in chapters 2 and 6.

More

There are two other metrics to share, and you can find them when you click on the More tab:

- Videos, which is in a beta stage—but it will give you data on how your videos are performing.
- Conversion tracking, which will allow you to convert websites for tracking purposes to measure events, gather audiences based on website behavior, and optimize marketing goals faster. It is definitely worth checking out after you get your bearings on Twitter metrics and usage first.

Now that you have a better understanding of what tool you can possibly use for your analyzing needs, let's take the time to discuss exactly what you are analyzing—these are called metrics. Metrics measure a certain type of data, and in this case, we are measuring all types of Twitter data. We have touched on this in previous sections when discussing the tools, but a more in-depth follow-up will ensure that you are capturing and analyzing the correct metrics for your engagement needs.

TWITTER METRICS TO ANALYZE

The basic metrics are as follows:

Followers

This metric gives you the data on how many followers you have gained over a certain period of time (a day, a week, a month); it will also show how many followers you have lost. Sometimes it is beneficial to measure this particular metric when you launch a campaign to gain followers, for example, if you start a campaign to gain one hundred followers over a month's period. You could use Twitter's built-in tool to measure if you are on target. If you decide to run a report every week, you will be able to see if you are on target or if you need to boost your strategy or tweak it in order to make your goal.

Posts

A post is a tweet that contains content; this can be a photo, video, or link as well. These will be considered posts with media. A post with just text or a quote of some kind is simply a post. Twitter recently increased the text amount for a tweet from 140 characters to 280 characters; it is still best to be brief and concise on Twitter but good to know that you can be a little more wordy if needed.

Replies

A reply is simply that—a reply to something that you posted; it is a direct reply to your post. If your tweets garner a lot of replies, this is usually a good indicator that you are engaging with your community. For example, if you are tweeting a link for a new collection at your library or a new exhibit at your museum, and your followers are engaging and asking questions about it through Twitter, this is a good way to see engagement strategies in action. But replies (or @ messages) can be something that you look at for negative comments or complaints regarding your library. If a follower or even a non-follower mentions your Twitter handle, it will appear in your replies, and it is best to view all of these tweets with caution, but if it is a valid comment or complaint, you can use it as an opportunity to further your engagement strategy. Replies, both negative and positive, are a surefire way to see engagement happening.

Retweets

A retweet is simply when a post is tweeted by another Twitter user. We use the abbreviation RT—it is a useful way to measure engagement, as it shows that your community values what you are tweeting and wants to spread the message of your content. For example, if your tweet about an author signing gets retweeted by the publisher of the book, the reach of your tweet has just increased, and your analytics will show different followers—and potential followers and groups to cater your feed toward in your future posts.

Likes/Favorites

That little heart button under the tweet is to signal that followers like/favorite your tweet. Like retweets, this is a good way to measure how well received your tweets are, and if you have a lot of likes/favorites for your tweets, this shows that many followers are enjoying and valuing your tweets, and it would be a good idea to continue posting similar tweets to continue that engagement trend.

Sprout Social delves deeper into Twitter metrics and suggests: "Content is a huge piece of your social media marketing strategy, but creating powerful content that delivers results requires data. When paid attention to, your Twitter metrics can have a major impact on what you get out of the social network" (Beese 2016).

Knowing the metrics that you want to keep track of, and what you need for goals and objectives for your own strategy, makes it worthwhile. Some libraries do not use any tools and simply rely on their own means of measure, and it works fine for their needs. You do not have to measure more advanced metrics and things that do not apply to your overall strategy.

For example, when Melissa Brisbin worked at the Cape May Library (@cmclibrary), she noted that "we haven't found an analytics tool to keep track of tweets. Retweeting would be only way to see if there's something popular." We heard a similar story from Lessa Pelayo Lozada, young readers librarian, at the Palos Verdes District Library (@pvld). She mentioned a similar strategy regarding analytic tracking, she noted "that (Palos Verdes District Library) keeps a mental tally of what is successful and what is not, as they are still in the beginning stages of developing a social media plan." Those are two examples of libraries that are using their own brand of tracking, but it does not mean you need to shy away from analytic tools. Do not feel that if you do not pay subscriptions for your data analytics that you cannot have a successful engagement strategy. Sure, there are plenty of great features that paid subscriptions can garner, such as real-time statistics, but do not feel defeated if your organization does not have the budget for it. You can measure and track your Twitter engagement with several free tools, including Twitter's own tool. The key to success is knowing what you are tracking and why you are tracking it to begin with; if you are just mindlessly tracking data with no focus, this will bring unnecessary work and trouble for your engagement strategy. Another way to track engagement without necessarily using tools would be to host a different type of participatory element and measure how well it does, for example, an Edit-a-Thon on Wikipedia, like the Jewish Museum (@TheJewishMuseum) recently hosted. The goal was to close the gender gap on

Wikipedia. They paired up with Art+Feminism (@artandfeminism) to make it happen. This is a good example of cross-promotion and how to track your engagement. Thinking of ideas like this for your library, archive, or museum can make the difference.

In our research on the value of studying analytics on Twitter, we found a few research studies on how to effectively analyze your Twitter data. In one research study, the authors compiled the most recent 1,200 tweets from the Twitter accounts of six U.S. public universities and concluded the categories or types of tweets: "The content analysis identified nine categories or types of tweets. The most frequently occurring type was event. . . . The second most frequently occurring category type was resource" (Stvilia and Gibradze 2014).

It is not surprising that event is the number one type of tweet as most Twitter presences serve as a broadcasting tool for promoting events and, yes, resources, which is the second most tweeted. A worthy note for the purpose of this book is that community building is third on the list in this study. The six other categories were operations update, study support, Q&A, survey, staff, and club. While it placed number three in this study, community building can be your number one, which means you can promote your library space as the nucleus of your community. In their findings, the distributions of the average number of retweets and favorites by tweet categories showed that study support and community building were the consistent top two for both retweets and favorites, based on their study design (Stvilia and Gibradze 2014). This definitely can support the concept that your strategy should include community building tweets. As noted in the study:

> The category community building included general tweets promoting the library as a place to receive research support, study or hang out and have fun. This category also included tweets providing emotional support and congratulating students on various achievements (e.g., completing exams), as well as congratulating the library or a specific department for being recognized or achieving a high ranking in a national poll. In general, these types of tweets used a higher rate of affective terms. (Stvilia and Gibradze 2014)

These types of tweets will continue to show your community the value that your organization can bring to their collective lives. If you are only tweeting about events, and never about how your organization may offer research support, you are missing the needs of your audience. Know what they need and reach out to them about it via Twitter.

Similarly, a study in the *Journal of Educational Multimedia and Hypermedia* compared the Twitter engagement and audience development of two museums for a six-month period (the two museums were the Hirshhorn Museum and Sculpture Garden @hirshhorn and the Smithsonian National Air and Space Museum @airandspace). It showed the majority of tweets were sharing links and resources. It is interesting to note that this is not necessarily a bad thing, but in terms of engagement analytics, the noteworthy findings were the low amount of ongoing conversation (Osterman et al. 2012). When looking at studies from different industries, the most successful are the ones that understand the importance of community engagement.

A good article primer to gather further thoughts on community engagement is an interview with Carrie Brown for the Center for News Excellence and Engagement. Carrie Brown (@brizzyc) is the director of social journalism at the Craig Newmark Graduate School of Journalism at the City University of New York (CUNY). In this interview with Anna Casey, Brown shares her definition of engagement journalism, which can apply beyond journalism and work with libraries, museums, and nonprofit organizations alike: "Rather than producing an article, video, or podcast, and then doing everything we can to convince people to look at it, we try to listen to the audience and understand their needs first" (Casey 2016).

This definition clearly helps to define what we intend to do when we use analytics—it is a way of listening to your community and seeing what works and what doesn't work. Analytics are a great way of seeing what your community needs. An added way of measuring what your community needs can be a survey or a focus group. These are both strong ways to get your community's voice into your engagement strategy. A survey could be a great way to build the engagement—starting with putting the call for survey participants on

Twitter and cross-promoting with other social media platforms to see how many cite Twitter as their entry point. Once you have a captive audience, you can ask and inquire about what they want to see on Twitter, what they need from Twitter, and so forth.

A Klipfolio article states:

> As important as it is for businesses to use Twitter to project a positive brand image and communicate with customers, like any social media platform, Twitter allows businesses to influence consumers, not control them. What this means is that businesses need to stay on top of external engagement in the "twitterverse" such as competitor profiles and brand awareness, just as much as internal Twitter metrics such as followers count and retweets. (Poleski 2016)

What this means for organizations as a whole is that it is important to look beyond metrics and actually engage in what your community is telling you directly. The line about influencing, not controlling, speaks volumes; it is the idea behind the whole notion of engagement at its core. Be an influence; be a part of the community. Do not dictate or remain above the community. When you conduct a survey, you are bringing the community into the decision process of your organization. This can also apply to a focus group—you can put the call out on Twitter for focus group participants. The difference with a survey and a focus group is the nature in which they are presented and asked. A survey is a set of questions and can be anonymous, if needed. With a focus group, you can cater the questions, and the anonymity factor is not there as they are done in person. Both can provide added engagement strategy tips and build on what your analytics have shown you in the reports and data.

Another study that showcases exactly what archivists are doing on Twitter notes that they are doing quite a lot:

> Through creative use of hashtags, a willingness to communicate with users and retweet relevant posts, and the availability of digital archival materials to share with their followers, archival institutions, as represented by the sample chosen for this study, are increasing access to and awareness of their collections. From bloggers who use historic images from the Vancouver Archives' digital collection to followers of the U.S. National Archives who learn about interesting events through their interaction with a NARA account, Twitter is home to a range of constructive activities and a potentially meaningful social network for archival institutions. (Kriesberg 2014)

This statement supports the idea that, in order for engagement to work, the community must be involved, and through analytics, you can build exactly what your community is asking for. Whether you are a librarian, an archivist, a digital strategist, a social media manager, or whatever title you hold, using analytics is the key to building engagement and understanding your community's needs.

Using analytics may be the last chapter of this book, but it is surely the beginning of crafting an engagement strategy that will succeed. Your strategy can work great for a few months and then things may fizzle and burn out, and you will need to look at the analytics to see what happened, where you should go from there, and how you can rework your social media strategy. Never look at it as fixed or unchangeable strategy; always be open to change and be willing to learn from your community—if you do not listen to them, if you do not engage with them, and if you are merely broadcasting and pushing content into the Twittersphere, your organization's Twitter presence will not succeed. If you need to refresh your strategy, reread or jump to chapter 1 to start the process over again.

REFERENCES

Beese, J. "A Deeper Look at the Twitter Metrics You Should Track." Sprout Social. 2016. sproutsocial.com/insights/twitter-metrics/.

Casey, A. "Professor Carrie Brown Shares Her Definition of Engagement Journalism." Center for News Excellence and Engagement. 2016. www.news-excellence.org/professor-carrie-brown-shares-her-definition-of-engagement-journalism/.

Kriesberg, Adam. "Increasing Access in 140 Characters or Less: Or, What Are Archival Institutions Doing on Twitter?" *The American Archivist* 77, no. 2 (Fall/Winter 2014): 534–557.

Osterman, M., M. Thirunarayanan, E. Ferris, L. Pabon, N. Paul, and R. Berger. "Museums and Twitter: An Exploratory Qualitative Study of How Museums Use Twitter for Audience Development and Engagement." *Journal of Educational Multimedia and Hypermedia* 21, no. 3 (July 2012): 241–255.

Poleski, D. "6 Must Have Metrics for Twitter Analytics." Klipfolio. 2016. www.klipfolio.com/blog/6-must-have-metrics-for-twitter-analytics/.

Stvilia, B., and L. Gibradze. "What Do Academic Libraries Tweet About, and What Makes a Library Tweet Useful?" *Library and Information Science Research* 36 (2014): 136–141.

Appendix A

University of Central Florida Libraries Social Media Guide

Reprinted with permission of the library.

WHY FOLLOW US

The UCF Libraries makes use of its various social media platforms to communicate library information, share interesting content, engage our community, and show our sense of humor.

WHERE TO FOLLOW US

Facebook—https://www.facebook.com/ucflibrary
Twitter—@ucflibrary
Instagram—@ucflibrary
Our Blog—http://library.ucf.edu/news/

SOCIAL MEDIA GOALS

Follow platform guidelines to build social media presence in a coordinated and consistent way. Welcome all UCF Libraries employees to contribute to sharing news and information through social media.

PLATFORM GUIDELINES

Facebook

- Community focus: UCF Libraries faculty/staff, campus and community partners, general audience

- Goal: Build a sense of community, show the library's personality, interact with our community
- Content for posts: Library announcements, shares of content related to libraries/reading in general, shares from our Instagram account & blog, time specific (St. Patrick's Day)
- Posting frequency: Twice daily
- Ongoing series: Dr. Pegasus
- Platform manager: Carrie Moran

Twitter

- Community focus: Students and faculty. Predominantly focused on undergraduate students. Campus and community partners.
- Goal: Expand dissemination of news and updates related to library services, events, collections, facilities, and campus involvement to encourage library "awareness" and usage. Remain active, professional, and friendly in responses to promote genuine and helpful library interaction experiences. Demonstrate the library's connection and support to the UCF campus and community at large.
- Content for posts: Announcements, events, services, new resources, campus highlights, and quirky/fun things related to libraries/reading/Dr. Pegasus/etc.
- Posting frequency: Daily total of 6 posts; 3 shares/retweets and 3 posts related to library and/or the campus and community.

- Ongoing series: Faculty/staff highlights/publications, 21st Century Library Project progress, What's Coming to the CFE Arena (i.e., post about a book related to the coming speaker), upcoming workshops, librarian quotes
- Platform manager: Cindy Dancel

Instagram

- Community focus: Campus and local Orlando area community; alumni
- Goal: Raise awareness of library resources (special/digital collections, spaces, etc.); build online community around library awareness (encourage active participation)
- Content for posts: university history, behind the-scenes in the library, campus and library events, important announcements (e.g., library hours, construction, etc.), collection highlights, library resources, and collaborations with campus/community partners
- Posting frequency: 1–2 times weekly (more if applicable)
- Ongoing series:
  o #libraryshelfie—features library shelves
  o #tbt—features SCUA
  o Humans of the UCF Library (users posing with books, library staff in action, #meetyourlibrarians, #librarylife)
- Platform manager: Carrie & SCUA rep

Blog

- Community focus: website visitors, engaged students, faculty & staff
- Goal: Show the library's personality while communicating library information to website visitors, sharing to social media and with specific user groups
- Content for posts: Generated from departments—events, announcements, news, features on a product/service
- Posting frequency: At least 1 post per week, ideally 2–4 posts per week
- Ongoing series: Humans of the UCF Library
- Platform manager: Web Working Group

Reddit

- Community focus: outliers, tech community
- Goal: Engage in discussions with our users, just in time information, feedback
- Content for posts: Announcements & asks for feedback
- Posting frequency: as needed
- Ongoing series: N/A
- Platform manager: Bobby

GLOBAL GUIDELINES

- Decisions about new platforms—from Social Media Committee under WWG, if other campus entities or academic libraries are using it, if users are talking about UCF Libraries on that platform; if the platform can be sustained by regular posts or updates from the Libraries; if number of users remains relatively high; platform "ownership" a consideration
- Shared Calendar
  o Events
  o Special days (Pi day, etc.)
  o Backup platform managers
- Emergency/Just in Time info
  o Communication with Administration (Meg as liaison to social media platform managers)
- E-mail distribution list for social media requests
- Awareness of other UCF social media efforts—Social Media Managers Group (at least one WWG Social Media team member will attend & make use of FB group), reciprocate on sharing content from other organizations
- We will monitor comments—and offensive or inaccurate comments will be deleted or corrected, as will commercial promotions.

STATISTICS

Facebook

- Followers: 4517 (as of 3/17/16)
- Interactions—190 comments, 1893 likes, 102 shares (from 8/3–12/19/2015)
- Top 20 engaging posts & Bottom 20 engaging posts—see appendix

Twitter

- Followers: 2015 (as of 3/17/16)
- Interactions: 9746 impressions over last 28 days (2/17–3/17/16)
- Top 20 engaging posts & Bottom 20 engaging posts—see appendix

Instagram

- Followers: 155 (total as of 3/17/16)
- Interactions: 788 likes received (ever)/47 comments received (ever)

- Top 20 engaging posts & Bottom 20 engaging posts—see appendix

Blog

- Followers—N/A, 4192 blog views 8/1/2015–12/31/2015
- Interactions—4 community comments, 5 staff comments (in response to posts, not other comments)
- Top 20 engaging posts & Bottom 20 engaging posts—see appendix

APPENDIX

Facebook Top 20 engaging posts (Oct–Dec 2015)

Post Message	Type	Lifetime Post Total Reach
The John C. Hitt Library has staff waiting to answer your questions today . . .	Photo	557
Vivian McCall—one of the UCF Libraries' most avid readers, curled up with . . .	Photo	604
Empty stacks on the third floor. We are making room for more quiet study . . .	Photo	608
Carnival of Open Access	Status	634
Congratulations to Dustyn Yost. He visited the John C. Hitt Library today . . .	Photo	639
In just ten minutes, STEP RIGHT UP to the UCF Open Access CARNIVAL!	Photo	664
Color Your Stress Away	Status	835
Congrats grads! We will miss you in the UCF Libraries. Come back and visit . . .	Link	923
Yesterday afternoon, Tuesday 8/25, the John C. Hitt Library was evacuated . . .	Link	1048
Our thoughts are with the family and friends of the young UCF student who . . .	Link	1086
What's your favorite quote from literature?	Shared Video	1194
Check out what the Washington Post had to say about UCF. #GoKnights . . .	Link	1205
Some choice tweeting from one of our favorite authors.	Photo	1737
Check out this list of 28 things that happen in the Wizarding World after . . .	Link	1794
The UCF Libraries is happy to welcome our newest librarian, CJ Ivory. On . . .	Photo	1842
The best of 30 years of Calvin & Hobbes.	Link	1900
Demie Donate, class of 2015, majored in Biology. After Commencement this	Photo	2338
A little literary humor for your morning.	Photo	2711
This has nothing to do with libraries, but is something we had to share!	Shared Video	3397
Come Color Your Stress Away! #ucflibrarycolors #ucf #ucflibrary #coloring . . .	Photo	3532

Facebook Bottom 20 engaging posts (Oct–Dec 2015)

Post Message	Type	Lifetime
Check out these ideas for a Thanksgiving Feast based on some of our . . .	Link	119
Richard Harrison, Librarian, recommends: City of Refuge: A Novel, by Tom . . .	Link	107
Try one of our audio books for your commute home! https://ucf.catalog.f...	Photo	72
What a great opportunity!	Photo	66
Bring your coven to the library today!	Photo	107
Open Access Policies: An Introduction from COAPI	Link	68
It's LGBT History Month! Check out the documentary "Trans" from the libr . . .	Link	180
UCF Library shared Special Collections & University Archives, UCF Libraries' . . .	Status	183
Don't be scared! Jump into some poetry this weekend with this list. And al . . .	Link	135

Post Message	Type	Lifetime
Critical Linking: November 15th, 2015	Link	259
Reminder that the UCF Library will be closed tomorrow in honor of Veteran' . . .	Status	44
Halloween + Books = A fun quiz to start your day! https://www.playbuzz . . .	Link	125
Are you an art or art history fan? View and download over 400 publication . . .	Link	75
It's Random Acts of Poetry Day! To a Young Poet Edna St. Vincent Millay . . .	Link	97
It's Monday, so you're probably going to spend part of your day daydream . . .	Link	103
The UCF Libraries would love to keep our undergrads around for another . . .	Link	108
Next time you're at the grocery, pick up a can of food or other high priority . . .	Photo	47
Great writing advice for anyone from award winning author Walter Dean . . .	Link	57
Infographic on famous books vs. their film adaptations http://www.fastco . . .	Link	67
Campus Connections is today! Come meet with the Office of Undergraduate . . .	Status	144

Twitter Top 20 engaging posts (Sep–Dec 2015)

Tweet Text	Category	Impressions
Happy 130th birthday to Rollins College! @OlinLibrary @rollinscollegeLibrary	Library Community	1224
Community1224Come Color Your Stress Away! #ucfibrarycolors #ucf #ucflibrary #coloring #stressrelief	Library Event	979
No need to race! Check computer availability before leaving your home https://t.co/8MZmi	Library Resource	880
Just a cute puppy to wish everyone a Happy Monday! https://t.co/Vp96yhG8ZZ	Fun	712
Rare library step stool graveyard. #ucflibrary #ucf #spooky @ UCF Library https://t.co/WM . . . ://t.co/WM	Library Photo	616
In 10 minutes, come to the CARNIVAL at the library! Games, prizes and plenty of props to . . .ge	Library Event	615
Get under the covers with a good book from our Knight Reads collection. #ucflibrary #knight	Library Resource	613
Come visit the UCF Library's Open Access Carnival tomorrow from 10-2PM in the John C . . . . Hi	Library Event	605
Will these be on your wish list? https://t.co/4t35QE3szY	Library Items	574
Don't live dangerously. For your protection, contact your friendly neighborhood librarian . . .	Library Services	566
The John C. Hitt Library is ready for the holidays. #UCF #ucflibrary #booktree #books #holidays	Library Photo	559
UCF Librarian @RayMulvy spotted at the Winter Park Arts Fest! https://t.co/Dje9gPDPGM	Librarian Photo	557
Come check out our newest exhibit "Art of Joy Postle" #ucflibrary #art #exhibit #joypostle #	Library Event	526

Tweet Text	Category	Impressions
FREE coffee or chocolate next wk for 15 minutes helping test our website. Email carrie.mora . . .	Library Event	525
Step right up to free food! Visit the Research and Information Desk on the main floor of the . . .	Library Event	500
We have a photo booth! And prizes! And free popcorn! Stop by before 2PM today! #UCFOAW	Library Event	470
Good Morning from the John C. Hitt Library. #goodmorning #ucflibrary #ucf #orlando . . . ori	Library Photo	465
Hey RobertDowneyJr ! @LindsayLynz is talking on the fourth floor of the library! We need . . .	Fun	464
Happy National Cat Day! To celebrate, Uber is delivering kittens! https://t.co/xsPgAACXhsh	Fun	463
The John C. Hitt Library looks great in the sunshine. #ucf #ucflibrary #orlando #florida . . . lib	Library Photo	445
Are you ready for Spirit Splash this week?!?! Take a look back at the ducks from our history . . .	UCF Event	444

Twitter Bottom 11 engaging posts (Sep–Dec 2015)

Tweet Text	Category	Impressions
@LindsayLynz Worth as hot!	Conversation with patron	79
@LindsayLynz *Fine print: Professional shusher may or may not resemble Robert Downey Jr.	Conversation with patron	132
@CEFLSTweets Thanks for the RT! Hope you're all having a great Thursday!	Thanks	147
@ LindsayLynz Sorry If it happens again, pls call 407-823-2580 & a professional shusher will be dispatched post haste! http://t.co/kCJL8pEfRY	Reply to complaint	160
@ gfdf_wdw @nanconnolly Thanks for the RTs guys! Hope everyone is enjoying their Wednesday!	Thanks	191
@ deborahbeckwin @rollinscollege Thanks for the RTs!	Thanks	208
#tbt UCF Libraries style. Anyone know who this handsome guy is? #ucflibrary #ucf #orlando #florida https://t.co/8nhdEr6Qj6	Library Collections	383

Tweet Text	Category	Impressions
Harry Potter Colouring Book from Studio Press http://t.co/qwuzcCjiFV via @ thebookseller	Harry Potter stuff	395
Empty stacks on the third floor. We are making room for more quiet study space on the fifth floor. https://t.co/mFB2nRQMZG	Library Photo	398
Follow the arrows to your fate. Fun, prizes, games, food and all FREE! #UCFOAWeek #OA #ucf #library https://t.co/iB8rKb8MFP	Library Event	417
Are you ready for Spirit Splash this week?!?! Take a look back at the ducks from our history on the https://t.co/50PCr3C7FF	Library Collections/UCF Event	444

Instagram Top 20 engaging posts (lifetime)

Instagram Bottom 20 engaging posts (lifetime)

Blog Top 20 engaging posts (8/1–12/31/15)

Page	Pageviews
/news/5th-floor-quiet-study-lounge/	155
/news/john-c-hitt-library-sorry-for-the-inconvenience/	152
/news/gameday-hours-9-3-15/	144
/news/the-seismic-shift-2015-is-over/	126
/news/group-study-rooms/	125
/news/publishing-in-the-academy-graduate-workshops-fall-2015/	111
/news/exhibit-artist-joy-postle-inspired-by-nature-1896-1989/	84
/news/exhibit-coming-soon-artist-joy-postle-inspired-by-nature-1896–1989/	81
/news/carnival-of-open-access-event/	77
/news/head-of-special-collections-university-archives-david-benjamin/	69
/news/todays-washington-post-ucf-storms-higher-education/	67
/news/knight-reads/	66
/news/employee-of-the-year-matt-desalvo/	59
/news/weekend-reading-08-28-15/	59
/news/general-collection-shift-in-john-c-hitt-library-2/	56
/news/jim-mauk-retires-after-35-years-at-ucf/	56
/news/game-day-hours-11-19-15/	55
/news/kram-for-the-exam-fall-15/	53
/news/new-books-at-the-rosen-library/	50
/news/shifting-finished-on-3rd-floor/	44

Blog Bottom 20 engaging posts (8/1–12/31/15)

Page	Pageviews
/news/weekend-reading-10-23-15/	21
/news/classrooms-open-for-studying/	17
/news/publishing-in-the-academy-summer-2015-library-research-workshops-for-graduate-students/	17
/news/elsevier-sciencedirect-personal-account-changes/	16
/news/national-society-of-minorities-in-hospitality-at-ucf-exhibit/	15
/news/weekend-reading-10-09-15/	14
/news/weekend-reading-10-16-15/	14
/news/american-civil-war-collection/	12
/news/sage-knowledge/	12
/news/stop-by-our-info-kiosk/	12
/news/kram-4-the-exam/	11
/news/weekend-reading-10-30-15/	11
/news/hathitrust-print-disabilities/	10
/news/shifting-project/	10
/news/10-most-read-asce-forensic-engineering-papers/	9
/news/gameday-hours-09-03-15/	6
/news/weekend-reading-11-20-15/	6
/news/carnival-of-open-access/	4
/news/stop-by-infokiosk/	4
/news/kram-for-the-exam-spring-15/	3

Appendix B

San Mateo County Libraries Social Media Procedures

Reprinted with permission of the library.

(1) SOCIAL MEDIA PROCEDURES

(a) **Purpose**

(i) The purpose of these procedures is to establish standards for and responsibilities regarding the authorized use by San Mateo County Library of social media. These standards ensure that SMCL staff using social media tools are compliant with existing policies and legal requirements. SMCL strives to use social media in advancing the organizational mission to provide innovative, dynamic services that connect our diverse community with opportunities for individual growth and enrichment. The use of social media supports organizational strategies to raise awareness of San Mateo County Library services and increase recognition of the library as an essential community asset.

(b) **Definition**

(i) Social media means any online platform for collaboration, interaction and active participation, including, but not limited to, social networking sites such as Facebook, Twitter, YouTube, LinkedIn and blogs. SMCL policy does apply to personal social media platforms that may be created by students, staff members, or other individuals that may sometimes include discussion of library-related issues but are not sponsored by SMCL.

(c) **Steps for Use of Social Media**
   (i) A Library that is looking to use social media or that is already using social media should be sure that it follows the following steps of use:
      o Consider whether and why it makes sense for your Library to use the particular social media outlet.
      o Realize that SMCL must approve new social media use. Please consider how current accounts/sites could be used to accomplish communications goals before opening a new account.
      o Using the template available from the Director's Office, Library Managers, or their designees, draft a Social Media Work Plan.
      o Submit the completed Social Media Work Plan to the Communications Manager in the Director's Office for review and recommendations.
      o A copy of the approved Social Media Work Plan shall be placed on file with the Communications Manager in the Director's Office.
      o Draft the Social Media Terms of Use to be used with the particular social media outlet using the available templates.
      o Submit the draft Social Media Terms of Use to your Library's Counsel for review.
      o Designate Library staff who will be responsible for the day-to-day use and maintenance of the service.
      o Create the social media presence for your Library, being sure to link to or post the Terms of Use on that service.
      o Make sure that Library staff both routinely monitor the social media outlet and

use the site for its intended purpose on a regular basis.
      o For any problems (such as people who post inappropriate content), work with the Communications Manager in the Director's Office to address the problem.
      o Comply with the other requirements of these procedures for the duration of the use of social media for official SMCL business.
      o Terminate use of social media outlet when the purpose has been fulfilled or the Library is no longer using the site.

(2) SOCIAL MEDIA POLICY

SMCL use of social media technology shall conform to the guidelines, responsibilities, and procedures contained or referenced in these procedures.

(a) **General Guidelines**
   (i) Each official SMCL presence on social media sites or services is considered an extension of the SMCL's information networks and is governed by SMCL policies, including e-mail, Internet usage, and portable computer policies.
   (ii) Official use by the Library of social media services is ultimately the responsibility of the Library Manager. Only authorized agents are permitted to conduct official SMCL business using social media sites and tools.
   (iii) Each Library must prepare a Social Media Work Plan and Terms of Use for each social media service it plans to use. The Work Plan and Terms of Use must be reviewed and approved as outlined by these procedures.
   (iv) Each Library Manager will ensure that the Library's designee(s) will routinely monitor content on each of the Library's social media services to ensure adherence to these procedures as well as message and branding consistent with the goals of SMCL.
   (v) Employees who publish to social media in the scope of their work for SMCL are acting

as representatives of SMCL via social media and accordingly must conduct themselves at all times in accordance with SMCL policies.

(vi) Libraries must keep, in a secure manner, an updated list of all user names and passwords associated with the Library's official social media accounts. It is important for the Library to have access to each account at any time in case of the unavailability of the person(s) who normally maintain each account, and the Library's designated users are required to update the Library with login information.

(vii) Libraries should never follow, like, or link to political campaign sites. While Libraries may "follow" or "like" the official social media accounts of elected officials, Libraries should exercise caution to avoid the appearance of endorsing a candidate or specific elected official and should not follow such officials' personal social media accounts not used for SMCL business.

(viii) Libraries may retweet, follow, like, share, and/or comment on posts by elected officials unless doing so would appear to endorse a political candidate or campaign. Libraries should also not use social media to take positions regarding political issues.

(ix) Libraries that use social media are responsible for complying with applicable federal, state, and county laws, regulations, and policies. This includes adherence to established law and policies regarding copyright, records retention, Public Records Act (PRA), First Amendment, and information security policies established by SMCL. These guidelines attempt to address the most common concerns in these regards.

(x) If a Library plans to collect contact information by way of social media services, it must do so by allowing members of the public to opt-in (rather than requiring them to opt-out of such collection), and it must include language in the Terms of Use regarding "Dissemination of Information" (this language is found in the available templates).

(b) Roles and Responsibilities

(i) The SMCL Director, or his/her designee, is responsible for setting policy guidelines.

(ii) The Communications Manager is responsible for facilitating these procedures in compliance with established SMCL rules and protocols. This includes responsibility to audit Library use of social media, to enforce policy compliance, to authorize social media tools/web sites prior to their use in the conduct of official SMCL business, and to review and provide feedback on occasion regarding social media use. Her/his role is to serve as a liaison between Libraries and the Director's Office to develop strategies to increase engagement on social media sites by collaborating with divisions, outlining a campaign calendar, creating relevant content, and conceptualizing tactics to grow audience participation.

(iii) The Communications Manager will keep a copy of all Libraries' Social Media Work Plans and maintain an understanding of which individuals are authorized by each Library to manage use of the Library's social media services. In addition, the Communications Manager will act as a resource to help Libraries develop appropriate uses for social media, identify the best social media tools to achieve their goals, define a strategy for community engagement using social media, and comply with social media best practices.

(iv) Library Managers have authority to establish and terminate social media use at the Library/division level and to set goals and practices regarding the Library's use of social media. The Library Manager has the duty to ensure that his/her employees are aware of the Social Media Policy and related policies and to take appropriate steps to enforce compliance, including establishing a well-thought out Social Media Work Plan that complements SMCL policies and considers SMCL's mission and goals.

(v) Social Media Manager. Each Library Manager shall designate at least one Social Media Manager for each of its uses of social media. The Social Media Manager shall have the authority to use social media on behalf of the Library and is responsible for ensuring the appropriateness of content in addition to complying with these procedures. The Social Media Manager shall ensure that the Library Manager or designee has up-to-date login information for its social media presence at all times.

(vi) The Director's Office is responsible for reviewing each Library's Terms of Use for each instance of social media use.

(3) PROCEDURES

(a) Requirements for Library's Use of Social Media

Libraries that choose to utilize social media shall:

(i) Establish a Social Media Work Plan that complements SMCL policies and considers the Library's mission and goals, audience, legal risks, technical capabilities, security issues, emergency response procedures, etc. The work plan shall be submitted to the Communications Manager for review and recommendations, with final approval by the Director.

(ii) Review the social media outlet's own Terms of Use and identify any items that would pose problems for the Library and/or SMCL. Counsel may be consulted with questions, but the Library must review and understand the site's Terms of Use.

(iii) Prepare the Library's Terms of Use document based on the templates available. The final Terms of Use shall be posted or linked on the social media platform being used.

(iv) Designate a Library Social Media Manager responsible for overseeing the Library's activity, policy compliance, and security protection for each social media platform being used.

(v) Be responsible for the creation, administration, and deactivation of social media accounts.

(b) Authorized Use

Library Managers, or designated Social Media Managers, are responsible for designating appropriate levels of use.

(i) Social Media Manager(s) (which may include official Library or program spokespersons), and Library Managers, or their respective designees, shall be considered authorized users and have permission to post and respond on behalf of the Library.

(ii) Appropriate usage levels include identifying what sites the Social Media Manager is approved to use, as well as defining capability for said use: publish, edit, comment, or view only.

(iii) To the extent that a Library Manager or designee authorizes other users to play an official role in relation to the Library's social media use, such authorized users shall review and comply with these procedures.

(iv) Social Media Manager(s) shall:
   1. be a SMCL employee;
   2. be familiar with SMCL policies;
   3. understand the scope of responsibility;
   4. and be appropriately trained to interact on behalf of a Library.

(c) Social Media Training

Once the Library has decided to engage in the use of social media, it will entrust specific individuals (Library Social Media Manager(s)) with the responsibility of posting and updating the Library's social media identity or page (e.g., writing the blog, updating the social networking page).

(i) Libraries must articulate clear expectations for its use prior to securing the social media identity or page.

(d) User Behavior

The same standards, principles and guidelines that apply to SMCL employees in the performance of their assigned duties apply to employees' work-related social media technology use.

(i) Authorized users shall only utilize their Library's social media accounts within the scope defined by their respective Library and in compliance with all SMCL policies, practices, user agreements, and guidelines.

(ii) Library Social Media Managers and all other authorized spokespersons participating in social networking discussions related to SMCL business matters on their personal social media accounts shall indicate that viewpoints are personal and do not necessarily reflect SMCL opinion.

(e) Approved Social Media Networks

Libraries shall only utilize SMCL-approved social media networks for official social media sites. Check with the Associate Management Analyst. SMCL will only sparingly approve new social media for programmatic initiatives. Proposals must show that current social media accounts/sites are not adequate.

(i) New social media networks under consideration will be reviewed and approved by the Director's Office and the SMCL's Communications Manager.

(ii) For each approved social media network, usage standards may be developed by the SMCL's Communications Manager to optimize government use of the site if necessary.

(f) Authenticity Establishment—Branding

Library/SMCL Program social media sites shall be created and maintained with identifiable characteristics of an official SMCL site that distinguishes them from non-professional or personal uses.

(i) SMCL social media network accounts shall be created using an official SMCL e-mail account.

(ii) Contact information should display an official SMCL e-mail address, include language regarding the fact that the account is the "official account," and provide a link to SMCL or Library website.

(iii) Use SMCL logo on social media accounts to confirm authenticity of site.

(iv) Terms of Use must be displayed. (See Creating the Terms of Use).

(v) Make sure your name includes some form of SMCL.

(g) Site Content

Libraries are responsible for establishing and maintaining content posted to their social media sites.

(i) Library Managers and/or Library Social Media Managers shall review site activity daily for exploitation or misuse.

(ii) Contents posted on SMCL social media sites may be considered public records subject to disclosure under California's Public Record Act ("PRA"—Government Code §§ 6250 et seq.). PRA requests for the production of posts on a SMCL social media site shall be referred to Counsel for review and response.

(iii) Sites or services shall include the text of or a link to the site-specific Terms of Use drafted by the Library and approved by Counsel as outlined below.

(iv) Unacceptable content (See: Updating Account Content: Unacceptable Content, in this document) shall be removed and repeat individual violators may, in some circumstances, be prohibited from further posting. Contact Counsel on any legal issues. (See: Retention of Records concerning content management and deletion.)

(v) Libraries shall have preventative measures in place against potential destructive technical incidents.

(h) Photo Guidelines

While patrons should not have an expectation of complete privacy while in a public space, SMCL should be conscious of not taking and posting photos to social media of individuals, especially minors, who are clearly identifiable (i.e., facial features are close and clearly visible, nametags visible with full name, etc.).

1) Ask the subject if it's OK to take and post his/her photo on social media.

2) If needed, have him/her sign a Media Release Form.

3) See Media Release Procedures for more information.

4) If reposting a patron's photo that contains minors who are clearly identifiable, please contact and ask if that's OK.

(i) Updating Account Content

Regularly: Libraries should develop a work plan to monitor accounts daily and update as appropriate for the type of site. For example, be prepared to post to Twitter a minimum once a day to build a following.

  (i) Emergency: Libraries should address use of social media during an emergency within their respective Library emergency operations plans.

 (ii) Dissemination and Interaction Tips:

   1. Monitor your social media network for discussion about SMCL, to reduce/eliminate inappropriate discussions/posts in accordance with the Terms of Use and these procedures.

   2. All SMCL accounts should be viewable to the public and should not use privacy settings.

   3. SMCL accounts should only join a group or become a fan of a page if it is related to work (can include professional, governmental or non-profit organizations).

   4. SMCL accounts can create their own groups by using the same guidelines mentioned in these procedures.

   5. **Acceptable Content** include, but are not limited to:
       i. Text;
      ii. Video and photographs—Be sure to check images and videos for sensitive information in the background and obtain releases as needed;
     iii. Graphics; and
      iv. Links (hyperlinks).

   6. **Unacceptable Content**. Only content that violates the Library's Terms of Use for a given social media service may be removed. The following are examples of content that may be prohibited by the Terms of Use and may be removed (with consultation of counsel) if appropriate:
       i. Profane language or content.
      ii. Explicit sexual or harassing content, including links to such content.

     iii. Violent or threatening content.
      iv. Solicitation of commerce, commercial activities, fund-raising or sponsorship.
       v. Illegal activity.
      vi. Information that may compromise the safety or security of the public or public systems.
     vii. Content that violates a legal ownership interest of any other party, such as trademark or copyright infringement.
    viii. Political activities by SMCL employees in an official capacity or the Library.
      ix. Posts by employees that violate SMCL or Library policies and procedures. Personal information about employees. Off-topic discussions or postings (for limited public forums).
       x. Making or publishing of false or defamatory statements concerning any individual.
      xi. Links that are primarily commercial in nature; or
     xii. Links that charge a user-fee for access.

   7. **Content Deletion**
       i. Unacceptable content should be removed as soon as possible. A copy of every deleted item must be retained. The following language can be used to warn individuals about their content: "Your recent post is in violation of SMCL's Social Media Policy and the library's Terms of Use for this social media service. SMCL reserves the right to remove, hide, or block such content. Please refrain from posting inappropriate content in the future. Thank you for your understanding."
      ii. Removing or blocking an individual from future posting on library Social Media page(s) is not recommended. Libraries should consult with assigned Counsel to determine

whether such action would be appropriate.

    iii. Tagged Material—Material that is tagged (via hash-tag, link to a Twitter account, link to a Facebook page, etc.) to Library accounts should be monitored to ensure appropriateness. If the tag violates these procedures or the Terms of Use, the Social Media Manager or designee shall remove the tag promptly.

Use a SMCL E-mail Account to Post

(i) To ensure that information posted on social media accounts is official, timely and accurate, all material posted should be tied either to the Library's official login or to the Library Social Media Manager's SMCL e-mail account. If needed, each Library should coordinate with the Director's Office and Technology to unblock social media from SMCL computers and to establish an appropriate e-mail account and URL or web address.

(k) Retention of Records

Library use of social media shall be documented and maintained in an easily accessible format that tracks account information, although the social media service itself may meet the requirements of retention. To the extent that the social media service only keeps information for a limited period, the Library should consult with its assigned Counsel regarding whether copies should be kept.

In general, the following guidelines should be followed:

(i) All content should be fully accessible to any person requesting documents from that site.

(ii) No records should be deleted without cause. Such removal must be done in compliance with the Terms of Use and policy. A copy of the removed material shall be retained in some manner.

(iii) Responsibility is left to each Library to retain records (refer to Technology and Counsel for suggestions).

(l) Security of Social Network

Libraries should take efforts to ensure that their use of social media is as secure as is reasonably possible in order to avoid unauthorized access to the social media account. The following strategies can minimize the risk of misuse of the account:

(i) Follow the best practices when setting secure passwords for social media sites.

(ii) Never leave station unattended or unlocked when logged on to a social media account.

(iii) Only Library Managers, or their designees, and the Library's Social Media Manager(s) should know login and password to social media account(s).

(iv) At least two people must have access to login credentials.

(v) If a Library's Social Media Manager changes, the login and password should also be changed or that person deleted from the list of site administrators.

(vi) In the event that social media use is compromised, the Library should immediately:

    1. Call Technology as soon as possible.

    2. If possible, change login and password information immediately.

    3. Acknowledge the security breach to social media followers in consultation with SMCL Communications Manager.

    4. Look for signs of damage, making necessary corrections.

    5. Report the incident to the Director's Office.

(4) GUIDELINES FOR EMPLOYEES

(a) At work: Employees or others affiliated with SMCL who use social media for SMCL-related business, including managing a Library's use of a social media service or posting comments in their official capacity, are required to comply with the following guidelines:

(i) You are Responsible for What You Publish. You are responsible for the content you publish on your Library social media site. Be mindful that what you publish will be public for a long time.

(ii) Stick to Your Area of Expertise. For example, it is not appropriate to comment on another county agency's or library's business. Instead, the moderator should direct the question to the appropriate Library. However, if you respond to a problem or issue, you need to own it. Once you become the point of contact for a patron or employee complaint, stay with it until it is resolved.

(iii) Considerations When Speaking on Behalf of Your Library. Identify yourself—name and, when relevant, role at your Library—when you discuss Library or Library-related matters on your Library's social media service or in connection with the Library's social media identity. Only speak on behalf of the Library when your commentary is based on your Library's explicit written standards, policies, and practices or when you have received prior permission from your supervisor to address a topic in a particular way. It is generally not appropriate for you to respond in an official capacity in relation to the Library's use of a social media service with your own personal views. You may respond in an official capacity using first person or passive voice if such a response is consistent with the Library's guidance regarding use of the social media service.

(iv) Understand Users' First Amendment Rights. Although a Library can moderate its social media services that accept comments from the public in order to restrict speech that is obscene, threatening, discriminatory, harassing, or off topic (if a limited public forum has been created), you may not use the moderation function to restrict speech with which the Library merely disagrees. Users have some First Amendment rights in posting content to public social media sites hosted or maintained by SMCL. Library moderators must respect those rights by not removing comments other than those excluded for specific legitimate reasons, such as those identified in the Library's Terms of Use.

(v) Do Not Comment on Social Media Sites Outside the SMCL's Social Media Sites or Identities. Do not publish content to any website or social media service outside of your Library's official website or social media service unless you have been authorized to do so by your Library Manager.

(vi) Respect Copyright Law. Social media participants must abide by laws governing copyright and fair use of copyrighted material owned by others. Never reprint whole articles or publications without first receiving written permission from the publication owner or confirming the copying is permitted. Never quote more than a short excerpt of someone else's work and, if possible, provide a link to the original. Also avoid posting content that contains photos, videos, music, or sound from another person or entity unless you have permission to re-post such material.

(vii) Protect Confidential Information. Do not provide confidential information or other protected information. Never post legally protected personal information that you have obtained from your Library (for example, information that is not public record). Ask permission to publish or report on conversations that occur within your Library. Never post information about policies or plans that have not been finalized by your Library unless you have received explicit permission from your supervisor to post draft policies or plans on the Library social media site for public comment. Never post photos or other information about clients, patients, or members of the public without confirming whether you are authorized to do so (See SMCL's Media Release Policy and Procedures).

(viii) Consider Your Content. As informal as social media services are meant to be, if they are being used in relation to SMCL, they can be official library communications. Social media services will be sought out by mainstream media, so a great deal of thought needs to go into how you will use the social media in a way that benefits both the Library and the public.

(ix) Don't Feed the Rumor Mill. Do not deny or confirm rumors or suggest either denial or confirmation in subtle ways. You may choose to respond by clarifying facts or let rumor-containing content stand without comment.

(x) Handling Negative Comments. Because the purpose of SMCL use of social media services is often to get input or feedback from the public, you should expect that some of the input or feedback will be negative. Some effective ways to respond to negative comments include:

(a) Providing accurate information in the spirit of being helpful

(b) Respectfully disagreeing

(c) Acknowledging that it is possible to hold different points of view

(d) However, negative comments that are not in violation of the Terms of Use should never be removed without first consulting Counsel.

(xi) Provide Links. When you make a reference to a law, regulation, policy, or other website, provide a link or a citation where possible.

(xii) Respect Your Audience and Your Coworkers. Don't use ethnic slurs, personal insults, or obscenity or engage in any conduct that would not be acceptable in your Library's workplace. Remember that SMCL's residents reflect a diverse set of customs, values, and points of view. You should also give proper consideration to privacy and be careful regarding topics that may be considered objectionable or inflammatory. By way of example, it is generally inappropriate for the government to take a stand on political or religious issues. Also, do not use your Library's social media presence to communicate among fellow SMCL employees. And do not air your differences with colleagues on your Library's social media's presence.

(xiii) Be Transparent and Differ Respectfully. Don't pick fights, be respectful in addressing input from the public with which you or the Library do not agree, and don't alter

previous posts without indicating that you have done so. When you see misrepresentations made about your Library by media or by other users, you may use the Library's social media site or identity to address the issue. However, you must do so with respect and should stick to the facts.

(xiv) Use the Social Media Site or Identity Only to Contribute to the SMCL Mission. When you contribute to your Library's social media site or identity, provide worthwhile information and perspective that contributes to your Library's mission of serving the public. What you publish will reflect on your Library and SMCL overall. Social media sites and identities should be used in a way that contributes to the Library's mission by:

(a) Helping you and your co-workers better perform your jobs;

(b) Informing patrons and partners about relevant information, services, and access;

(c) Making the operations of your Library transparent and accessible to the public;

(d) Creating a forum for the receipt of input from residents; and

(e) Encouraging civic engagement.

(xv) Respond to Your Own Mistakes. If you make an error, own up to it and correct it quickly. In general, only spelling errors or grammar fixes should be made without making the change evident to users. If you choose to modify an earlier post, make it clear that you have done so, and do not remove or delete the incorrect content without providing the correct information and acknowledging the change. Ways to accomplish this include:

(a) Strike through the error and correct it; or

(b) Create a new post with the correct information and link to it from the post you need to correct or clarify. Either method is acceptable. The goal is for the Library's social media use to achieve transparency.

(xvi)   Use Your Best Judgment. If you're about to publish something that makes you even the slightest bit uncomfortable, review the suggestions above and think about why that is. If you're still unsure, discuss it with your manager.

(xvii) Respect Your Time. Make sure that your online activities, even if they are sanctioned or required by your Library, do not interfere with other parts of your job. Employee social media users are responsible for keeping their managers informed about any social media duties that may be interfering with their jobs.

(xviii) Handling Media Inquiries. A Library's social media use may lead to increased inquiries from the media. If you are contacted directly by a reporter, you should refer media questions to your Library's designated media contact and/or the Communications Manager.

(b) Using Social Media Outside of Work

(i)   These social media guidelines for SMCL employees have been created to address some of the choices that individual employees, contractors, consultants, temporary staff and other workers at SMCL may face online. These guidelines are not intended to address every situation encountered through use of social media.

(ii) Whether or not a SMCL employee chooses to create or participate in a blog, wiki, online social network or any other form of online publishing or discussion outside the workplace is his or her own decision. However, emerging online collaboration platforms are fundamentally changing the way SMCL employees work and engage with each other, clients and partners. The old social norms and standards still apply, but the openness of social media creates situations that call for new rules of etiquette.

(a) Employee's personal use must not be attributable to the Library or employee's job function at Library. While an employee's use and comments made at social media sites are subject to First Amendment protections, as well as permissible restrictions, any personal use made of social media sites outside of work must not be attributable to the Library or the employee's job function at the agency. For example:

1. Do not use your work e-mail address to register for social media and other sites unless the purpose is directly related to your job.

(iii) Do not display the SMCL logo or other official logos on personal social networking accounts.

(iv)   Don't provide the SMCL's or another's confidential or other proprietary information.

(v)   Do not state or imply that you speak for SMCL, for a Library, or for library officials.

(vi)   Protect your privacy. Employees are personally responsible for the content they publish on blogs, wikis or any other form of user-generated media. SMCL is not responsible for the personal content of your social media sites. Be mindful that what you publish may be public for a long time. Be aware of your association with SMCL in online social networks. If you identify yourself as a SMCL employee, ensure your profile and related content is consistent with how you wish to present yourself with colleagues and clients.

(vii) Use a disclaimer. Whether you publish to a blog or some other form of social media, make it clear that what you say there is representative of your views and opinions and not necessarily the views and opinions of SMCL. Unless you are specifically authorized by your manager or supervisor to speak on behalf of SMCL, consider including the following disclaimer on personal blogs or social media in which you identify yourself as an SMCL employee: "The postings on this site are my own and don't necessarily represent SMCL's positions, strategies or opinions."

(5) SOCIAL MEDIA LEGAL ISSUES

(a) Social media use implicates many legal issues. In order to protect each Library and SMCL from unwanted problems, each Library considering utilizing social media must review the following points/issues (listed in Part 1, below), present a summary of its anticipated use with respect to these legal issues in its Social Media Work Plan (requirements listed in Part 2, below), and then finalize the Terms of Use with respect to the use of that particular social media resource for posting on or linking from the social media service before utilizing the social media. The Library should contact the Director's Office with questions or concerns about these or other legal issues.

(b) Part 1—Legal Concerns:

   (i)   In preparing to use social media services, a Library should consider each of the following topics before making a decision to use the service and keep these points in mind when drafting its Work Plan:

      1. The Site's Terms of Use. Libraries utilizing social media resources should be aware that each site or resource likely has its own terms and conditions of use, and some of those terms and conditions may create a conflict with SMCL policies. Each Library must review the terms and conditions of use for each site or resource it plans to use and address any issues they spot in the legal discussion section of the work plan during the planning stage. It is the Library's responsibility to understand the site's restrictions and rules.

      2. Where the Terms of Use implicate a legal issue, Counsel will provide input to the Library regarding ways to address the issue or counsel the Library on the risks it is assuming in utilizing the social media resource.

      3. Other Legal Issues. Aside from the content of a particular social media outlet's Terms of Use, there are a number of general concerns that must be addressed by the Library. Below is a summary of the key concerns the Library must consider, and the Library must create a Terms of Use document from one of the provided templates to address these items. The text of the Terms of Use adopted by the Library must be posted or linked on the Library's social media presence. Your assigned Counsel must review and approve the Terms of Use and can provide further information about the issues.

      4. The list of issues, which is subject to modification, includes the following:

        i. First Amendment Concerns. The United States and California Constitutions protect the freedom of speech of citizens from undue restrictions by the government. Because SMCL and its Libraries are government actors, the ways in which they can limit speech are restricted by these constitutional protections, including the First Amendment.

      5. To the extent that social media outlets permit users other than the Library to generate content (such as by posting comments), the Library must carefully decide whether to permit such user-generated content. If a Library's use of a site is only informational, such as using a site to disseminate information without permitting comments by other participants, the Library may list information that would be appropriate for sharing with the public. However, if the Library decides to use the site to permit user-generated content (i.e., content from outside the Library) to be posted or shared, First Amendment issues can come into play.

      6. In order to protect SMCL, the Library must adopt one of the following designations for its use of the social media and follow the accompanying requirements below before beginning its use of

the social media site or resources. Any planned change to the type of use by the Library must be made in consultation with Counsel and must also be made in accordance with these categories and requirements before such change is made. The categories are:

i. Information sharing only: If the use of the site/resource involves only sharing of information by the Library, with no posting of information by anyone other than authorized Library representatives, then the use of the site or resource is considered "information sharing" and does not create any kind of public forum. This is true even if others can send messages to the Library through the resource or site. So long as such messages are not posted for others to view, the use remains "information sharing" only. Creating a list of information based on input from others, such as a public list of frequently asked questions, does not turn the use into a public forum.

ii. Non-public forum: If the Library wishes to create a limited, non-public forum for use by a small set of individuals, such as by Library employees only, it can impose restrictions on the kinds of topics it wishes to encourage input on or even can limit the types of views on the topic that are permitted. To the extent that social media resources are used for this purpose, the Library should limit access to the intended users so as to avoid permitting authorized users to have comments broadcast to the general public, thus destroying the non-public nature of the forum. The level of control associated with this kind of non-public forum requires clear restrictions determined in advance regarding the limits on con-

tent and that prevent general access. As with public forums below, the restrictions on topics or even on particular viewpoints should be clear, objective, and uniformly applied.

iii. Public forum: If the Library opts to permit comments, feedback, or other information to be posted by anyone other than the Library representative(s) for viewing by the public or other users, the Library may be creating a public forum of some kind. The ability of the Library to limit, alter, or remove such comments, feedback, or other information depends on the policies adopted by the Library prior to allowing such content.

7. In no event should the Library engage in discrimination based on the viewpoint expressed in such comments, feedback, or other information. Once the forum is opened to participation by the public, the Library must remain viewpoint neutral. However, there are ways in which the Library can limit or control the content of such forums. Also, the Library must be clear to users about the type of forum it is creating, indicate any limits on the types of content allowed in clear, unambiguous terms, and be consistent in the application of those limits on all comments, feedback, or other information. Accordingly, the Library must decide which of the following types of forums it wishes to create:

i. Designated public forum: If the Library wishes to allow substantial input from others with minimum restrictions, it can create a designated public forum. In general, a designated public forum only permits content-neutral limitations on the kind of speech. So a Library could limit the timeframe during which comments on a particular topic are permitted, or it could restrict all comments to a certain length. In order to limit the kinds of views expressed, the Library would need to show that the restrictions are necessary to serve a compelling government interest and that the restriction is narrowly drawn to achieve that end. Such restrictions can be hard to draft, and accordingly a Library should create a designated public forum with caution. In creating such a forum, the Library is generally limiting its own ability to remove content that may be deemed divisive, upsetting, or even off-topic.

ii. Limited public forum: If the Library wishes to allow input from others that is limited to specific topics, it can create a limited public forum. In general, although a limited public forum still only permits content-neutral limitations on the kind of speech, it does allow for speech to be restricted to certain topics. For example, a Library could create a forum for others to post questions regarding a particular subject matter. So long as the Library is clear about the topical restrictions and is uniform in its enforcement, the Library has the ability to remove comments that are off-topic. However, the Library should still be aware that it will need to leave in place comments that, although perhaps off-color and non-productive, still relate to the topic. So, if the Library asks for questions regarding its policies for dealing with the public, and someone posts a facetious question that suggests the Library Manager has no interest in dealing with the public, that comment should not be removed. When in doubt about whether a comment can be removed, the Library should consult with Counsel. To help create a limited public forum, the Library should avoid subjective or overly general criteria regarding the subject-matter limitations. The more limited, more objective, and more specific the criteria is, the better. Also, the Library should consider whether it wants to restrict participation using objective criteria (e.g., limiting participation to employees or certain groups of constituents) or utilize administrative control over access to the forum. Both such controls can help create a secure limited public forum. Also, in a limited public forum, policies against "personal attacks" may be permissible so long as the limitation is reasonably necessary to encourage public participation and foster discussion of the issues for which the forum was created.

iii. For any forum created by the Library, the Library must post the applicable information listed below on the social media website, must consistently apply its guidelines to all comments, and must utilize objective and specific criteria for limiting comments, as outlined below.

iv. Also, although social media sites might have their own policies restricting users in their speech (such as limits on use of profanity or personal attacks), the Library should avoid enforcing the social media outlet's rules in these areas. The Library can enforce its own Terms of Use, but if other users have concerns about a violation of the social media outlet's terms or conditions, such users should be directed to the social media outlet directly. This will help avoid problems where a comment may constitute permitted First Amendment speech (and therefore should not be removed by SMCL) but may be removed by the site itself (which the site can do based on its own terms or conditions of use).

8. Public Meeting Requirements (the Brown Act): The Ralph M. Brown Act (Gov. Code, § 549501 et seq.) governs meetings conducted by local legislative bodies, such as boards of supervisors, city councils, and school boards. The purpose of the Brown Act is to facilitate public participation in local government decisions and to curb misuse of the democratic process by secret legislation by public bodies, and the Brown Act imposes an "open meeting" requirement on local legislative bodies. The Act only applies to multi-member bodies such as councils, boards, commissions and committees, which are created for the purpose of reaching collaborative decisions through public discussion and debate. For purposes of social media, Libraries must remain aware that the Brown Act applies to meetings of a majority of the members of such multi-member bodies, including "serial meetings," which can be held when members collect information or conduct business by communication in sequence, such as by e-mail or the Internet. The Library should avoid having its use of social media create a meeting of such multi-member bodies, and when in doubt the Library should contact Counsel. More information on the Brown Act is available online at: ag.ca.gov/publications/2003_Intro_BrownAct.pdf.

9. Public Records Act: Information posted by the Library on social media, including information the Library permits to be posted by other users, may be subject to the Public Records Act. To the extent such social media outlets are open to the public, the public by definition already has access to those records and can access them without the assistance of the Library or SMCL. However, the cautionary language in the Terms of Use templates should be used by the Library on the site/service. In addition, the Library should consider whether it wants to archive information from the site for any reason.

10. Dissemination of Information and Spam/Text Messaging: The Library should avoid sending spam by way of social media, unless participants have opted-in to notifications of some kind. In addition, the Library should never send unsolicited text messages to mobile telephone devices as doing so is against the law. If the Library plans to collect contact information from social media participants to use to disseminate information, the Library must: (1) post its policy regarding authorized uses of the distribution list; (2) require subscribers to opt-in to the list; (3) permit subscribers to remove themselves from the list at any time by contacting a listed representative of the Library; (4) not release the list of subscribers except as authorized by law; and (5) not use the list except as outlined in the Library's posted policy regarding use of the list.

11. Intellectual Property: The Library shall avoid using the intellectual property (trademarks, artwork, music, other protected symbols or copy-written materials) of other individuals or organizations unless expressly authorized by the owner to use the protected intellectual property.

12. Advertising: Many social media services use contextual advertising that is not within the control of the Library. Accordingly, the policy statement in the Terms of Use templates regarding advertising should be included in the Library's policies on the site/service.

(c) Part 2—Creating a Social Media Work Plan: In preparing its Social Media Work Plan, the Library should include discussion of how each of the legal issues raised above will come into play, if at all, in relation to its planned use of the social media resources being considered. There is no specific format for drafting this discussion, but the Library can use the topics from Part 1, above, as an outline for addressing the legal issues. The summary should also indicate which type of forum, if any, the Library's use will create in relation to the First Amendment concerns listed above. The Library can then address the other legal issues listed, and it can simply state that certain issues are not implicated if that is the case. SMCL's Counsel may be consulted with any questions at this stage of the process. The Director's Office will make available a template for creating a Work Plan.

(d) Part 3—Creating the Terms of Use: Based on the issues outlined above, the Library should determine which kind of First Amendment forum it wishes to create. Once it makes that decision, the Library should draft the Terms of Use it will link to or post on the social media site using one of the four templates available on the intranet via the Social Media Handbook. There is one template for each type of First Amendment Forum. The draft Terms of Use document must then be sent to SMCL Counsel for review, input, and approval. Once it is approved you must post the document to the social media service (or make a link to it clearly visible to users of the social media service).

(6) TERMS OF USE TEMPLATES

(a) Once you have confirmed that which is the right template for the type of forum you plan to create, please fill out/complete all sections below listed in [brackets]. One you have completed this template, forward to the Director's Office/Communications Manager. After the terms of use are final, you can then copy-and-paste them into an appropriate location on the social media site. For example, in Facebook, you can create a tab on the left of a "fan page" for "Terms of Use" and paste the text into the portion for that section. ***Likely, most Library social media sites will be considered Limited Public Forum***

(b) Full Public Forum
    1. Terms of Use
    2. Purpose: The [Library name] has decided to use this site/service for the pur-

pose of [insert purpose, being as specific as possible]. The [Library name]'s use of this site/service is being done as deemed advisable by that Library, which may decide to change or eliminate its use of this site/service.

3. Limitations on Use: It is the intent of [Library name] to create a designated (full) public forum with its use of this site/service in relation to the purpose(s) listed above. As part of the Library's efforts to further these purposes, the comments section of this site/service is being offered as a designated public forum intended to serve as a mechanism for communication between the public and the Library with respect to [list purposes or state "the purpose(s) listed above"]. Participation by other users is accordingly not limited to specific subject matters or topics.

4. However, with respect to such comments, the Library reserves the right to remove inappropriate comments, including those that have obscene language or sexual content, involve ad hominem personal attacks on another user, threaten or defame any person or organization, violate the legal ownership interest of another party, promote illegal activity, or promote or solicit commercial services or products. The Library believes these restrictions to be reasonably necessary to encourage public participation and foster discussion by maintaining a civil discourse and permitting all differing viewpoints.

5. [Library name] will routinely monitor the comments posted by other users of this site/service, and any comments that are not in line with these restrictions will be removed. To the extent that any user believes the comments of another user are not in line with these purposes and restrictions, they are welcome to notify [Library name] by [method]. [Library name] will make

a determination about the appropriateness of such comments based on its application of these purposes and restrictions, and that determination is final and not subject to outside review. [Library name] intends its application of these purposes and restrictions to be made in a manner that is viewpoint neutral and is consistent over time. [Library name] intends for this forum to become an open avenue for public discourse. Please note as well that any terms of service that this site/service places on user participation still apply to comments made by any user, and this site/service may enforce its own terms of service. To the extent that any user believes a comment has been made in violation of the terms of service of this site/service, that person should contact the site/service rather than contacting [Library name], as [Library name] has no obligation to enforce the terms of service of this site/service.

6. Statement Regarding Terms of Use and Privacy: Use of this site/service is subject to the terms of use of the site/service, including the privacy policies of the site/service, which can be found here: [insert link to the website's terms of use (for example, www.facebook.com/terms.php)]. Anyone posting comments or submitting information to [Library Name] on this site/service should keep this in mind. In addition, the poster of comments or information to this site/service agrees that his or her comments may be treated by the SMCL as a public record subject to disclosure pursuant to Cal. Gov't Code Section 6250 et seq., regardless of whether such comments actually constitute a public record. Posters are urged to protect their privacy and should consider refraining from posting personally identifying information, including but not limited to: last name, address, age, and phone number. To the extent this site/service is open to the public, the public has access to its content and can access that content without the assistance of the Library or the SMCL.

7. Responsibility for Content: Except for information disseminated by the owner/manager of this [blog, fan page, etc.], any information posted or submitted by others expresses the views of the person submitting such information and not necessarily the views of SMCL or the Library, and neither SMCL nor the Library is responsible for the opinions and information shared by others.

8. Disclaimer of Notice: Communications made through this site/service shall in no way be deemed to constitute legal notice to the SMCL or any of its agencies, officers, employees, agents, or representatives with respect to any existing or potential claim or cause of action against SMCL or any of its agencies, officers, employees, agents, or representatives where notice to SMCL is required by any federal, state or local law, rule or regulation.

9. Advertising: Users of this site/service should understand that contextual advertising as appears on this site/service is byproduct of use of the site/service. [Library name] does not control the site or service's placement or use of such advertising, and in no way does the use by [Library name] of this site or service constitute any endorsement or support of any such advertisements. Reference in such advertisements or in any user-generated content herein to any specific commercial products, process, or service by trade name, trademark, manufacturer, or otherwise does not constitute or imply endorsement, recommendation, or favoring by the SMCL, and the Library's use of this site/service shall not be used for advertising or product endorsement purposes.

10. Contact Person: You may contact [Library name] via [insert preferred method, whether through the message option of the site/service or other option, listing a name or position title as appropriate]. In addition, [Library name] may be contacted by telephone at [add main Library number].

    (a) In addition, if the Library plans to collect contact information by way of the site/service allowing users to opt-in to announcements, it must draft a section titled "Dissemination of Information," as follows. If the Library needs assistance, it should contact Counsel for help drafting this section. The section should read as follows:

11. Dissemination of Information: [Library name] will allow users/subscribers to opt-in to receiving information or notifications in relation to the Library's use of this site. The Library will only use the list for dissemination of the following kinds of information for the following purposes: [insert description of information to be disseminated and purposes of distribution]. Users/subscribers that are interested in receiving information or announcements on a periodic basis must opt-in to receiving such information, and subscribers are permitted to remove themselves from the announcement list at any time by contacting the listed representative of the Library. The Library will not release the list of subscribers except as authorized by law, and the Library will not use the list except as outlined in the Library's posted policy regarding use of the list.

(c) Limited Public Forum

    1. Terms of Use
    2. Purpose: The [Library name] has decided to use this site/service for the purpose of [insert purpose, being as specific as possible]. The [Library name]'s use of

this site/service is being done as deemed advisable by that Library, which may decide to change or eliminate its use of this site/service.

3. Limitations on Use: It is the intent of [Library name] to create a limited public forum with its use of this site/service for the purpose(s) listed above. As part of the Library's efforts to further these purposes, the comments feature of this site/service is being offered as a limited public forum intended to serve as a mechanism for communication between the public and the Library with respect to [list purposes or state "the purpose(s) listed above"]. Comments will be restricted in the following manner: [list viewpoint-neutral restrictions, being as specific as possible, such as "comments will be limited to 500 words"; "comments will be permitted only until January 15, 2012"; and/or "comments will be limited to the following topics: [list topics]"].

4. With respect to such comments, the Library reserves the right to remove inappropriate comments, including those that have obscene language or sexual content, involve ad hominem personal attacks on another user, threaten or defame any person or organization, violate the legal ownership interest of another party, promote illegal activity, promote or solicit commercial services or products, or are not topically related to the particular posting/permitted subject matters. The Library believes these restrictions to be reasonably necessary to encourage public participation and foster discussion of the issues for which the forum was created by maintaining a civil discourse and permitting all differing viewpoints on the approved topics.

5. [Library name] will routinely monitor the comments posted by other users of this site/service, and any comments that are not in line with these restrictions will be removed. To the extent that any user

believes the comments of another user are not in line with these purposes and restrictions, they are welcome to notify [Library name] by [method]. [Library name] will make a determination about the appropriateness of such comments based on its application of these purposes and restrictions, and that determination is final and not subject to outside review. [Library name] intends its application of these purposes and restrictions to be made in a manner that is viewpoint neutral and is consistent over time. [Library name] does not intend for this forum to become a fully open avenue for public discourse but rather is using this site/service for discussion of a limited nature. Please note as well that any terms of service that this site/service places on user participation still apply to comments made by any user, and this site/service may enforce its own terms of service. To the extent that any user believes a comment has been made in violation of the terms of service of this site/service, that person should contact the site/service rather than contacting [Library name], as [Library name] has no obligation to enforce the terms of service of this site/service.

6. Statement Regarding Terms of Use and Privacy: Use of this site/service is subject to the terms of use of the site/service, including the privacy policies of the site/service. Anyone posting comments or submitting information to [Library Name] on this site/service should keep this in mind. In addition, the poster of comments or information to this site/service agrees that his or her comments may be treated by SMCL as a public record subject to disclosure pursuant to Cal. Gov't Code Section 6250 et seq., regardless of whether such comments actually constitute a public record. Posters are urged to protect their privacy and should consider refraining from posting personally identifying information, including but not limited to: last name, address, age, and phone number. To the extent this site/service is open to the public, the public has access to its content and can access that content without the assistance of the Library or SMCL.

7. Responsibility for Content: Except for information disseminated by the owner/manager of this [blog, fan page, etc.], any information posted or submitted by others expresses the views of the person submitting such information and not necessarily the views of SMCL or the Library, and neither SMCL nor the Library is responsible for the opinions and information shared by others.

8. Disclaimer of Notice: Communications made through this site/service shall in no way be deemed to constitute legal notice to SMCL or any of its agencies, officers, employees, agents, or representatives with respect to any existing or potential claim or cause of action against SMCL or any of its agencies, officers, employees, agents, or representatives where notice to SMCL is required by any federal, state or local law, rule or regulation.

9. Advertising: Users of this site/service should understand that contextual advertising as appears on this site/service is byproduct of use of the site/service. [Library name] does not control the site or service's placement or use of such advertising, and in no way does the use by [Library name] of this site or service constitute any endorsement or support of any such advertisements. Reference in such advertisements or in any user-generated content herein to any specific commercial products, process, or service by trade name, trademark, manufacturer, or otherwise does not constitute or imply endorsement, recommendation, or favoring by SMCL, and the Library's use of this site/service

shall not be used for advertising or product endorsement purposes.

10. Contact Person: You may contact [Library name] via [insert preferred method, whether through the message option of the site/service or other option, listing a name or position title as appropriate]. In addition, [Library name] may be contacted by telephone at [add main Library number].

 (a) *In addition, if the Library plans to collect contact information by way of the site/service allowing users to opt-in to announcements, it must draft a section titled "Dissemination of Information," as follows. If the Library needs assistance, it should contact County Counsel for help drafting this section. The section should read as follows:*

11. Dissemination of Information: [Library name] will allow users/subscribers to opt-in to receiving information or notifications in relation to the Library's use of this site. The Library will only use the list for dissemination of the following kinds of information for the following purposes: [insert description of information to be disseminated and purposes of distribution]. Users/subscribers that are interested in receiving information or announcements on a periodic basis must opt-in to receiving such information, and subscribers are permitted to remove themselves from the announcement list at any time by contacting the listed representative of the Library. The Library will not release the list of subscribers except as authorized by law, and the Library will not use the list except as outlined in the Library's posted policy regarding use of the list.

(d) Non-Public Forum
  1. Terms of Use
  2. Purpose: The [Library name] has decided to use this site/service for the pur-

pose of [insert purpose, being as specific as possible]. The [Library name]'s use of this site/service is being done as deemed advisable by that Library, which may decide to change or eliminate its use of this site/service.

3. Limitations on Use: It is the intent of [Library name] to create a non-public forum with its use of this site/service for the purpose(s) listed above. As part of the Library's efforts to further these purposes, the comments feature of this site/service is being offered to a limited group of individuals with restricted access to the information as a non-public forum intended to serve as a mechanism for communication between the group members and the Library with respect to those purposes.

4. Participation by users is limited to [describe restriction on participants, using objective criteria (e.g., limiting participation to employees or certain groups of constituents). And the owner of this page will also use [insert method, such as requiring a County-assigned ID/password to access the site, restricting comments to County IP addresses, etc.] to impose administrative control over access to the forum. Finally, [Library name] will remove any comments, including comments on the approved topics, that [add content-based and/or neutral restrictions, which should be clear, objective, and uniformly applicable].

5. With respect to such comments, the Library reserves the right to remove inappropriate comments, including those that have obscene language or sexual content, involve ad hominem personal attacks on another user, threaten or defame any person or organization, violate the legal ownership interest of another party, promote illegal activity, promote or solicit commercial services or products, or are not topically related

to the particular posting/permitted subject matters. The Library believes these restrictions to be reasonably necessary to encourage participation and foster discussion of the issues for which the forum was created by maintaining a civil discourse and permitting all relevant viewpoints on the approved topics.

6. [Library name] will routinely monitor the comments posted by authorized users of this site/service, and any comments that are not in line with these restrictions will be removed. To the extent that any authorized user believes the comments of another user are not in line with these purposes and restrictions, they are welcome to notify [Library name] by [method]. [Library name] will make a determination about the appropriateness of such comments based on its application of these purposes and restrictions, and that determination is final and not subject to outside review. [Library name] intends its application of these purposes and restrictions to be consistent over time. [Library name] does not intend for this forum to become an avenue for public discourse. Please note as well that any terms of service that this site/service places on user participation still apply to comments made by any user, and this site/service may enforce its own terms of service. To the extent that any user believes a comment has been made in violation of the terms of service of this site/service, that person should contact the site/service rather than contacting [Library name], as [Library name] has no obligation to enforce the terms of service of this site/service.

7. Statement Regarding Terms of Use and Privacy: Use of this site/service is subject to the terms of use of the site/service, including the privacy policies of the site/service, which can be found here: [insert link to the website's terms of use (for example, www.facebook.com/terms.php)]. Anyone posting comments or submitting information to [Library Name] on this site/service should keep this in mind. In addition, the poster of comments or information to this site/service agrees that his or her comments may be treated by SMCL as a public record subject to disclosure pursuant to Cal. Gov't Code Section 6250 et seq., regardless of whether such comments actually constitute a public record. Posters are urged to protect their privacy and should consider refraining from posting personally identifying information, including but not limited to: last name, address, age, and phone number. To the extent this site/service is open to the public, the public has access to its content and can access that content without the assistance of the Library or SMCL.

8. Responsibility for Content: Except for information disseminated by the owner/manager of this [blog, fan page, etc.], any information posted or submitted by others expresses the views of the person submitting such information and not necessarily the views of SMCL or the Library, and neither SMCL nor the Library is responsible for the opinions and information shared by others.

9. Disclaimer of Notice: Communications made through this site/service shall in no way be deemed to constitute legal notice to SMCL or any of its agencies, officers, employees, agents, or representatives with respect to any existing or potential claim or cause of action against SMCL or any of its agencies, officers, employees, agents, or representatives where notice to SMCL is required by any federal, state or local law, rule or regulation.

10. Advertising: Users of this site/service should understand that contextual advertising as appears on this site/service is byproduct of use of the site/service. [Library name] does not control the site or service's placement or use of such advertising, and in no way does the use by [Library name] of this site or service constitute any endorsement or support of any such advertisements. Reference in such advertisements or in any user-generated content herein to any specific commercial products, process, or service by trade name, trademark, manufacturer, or otherwise does not constitute or imply endorsement, recommendation, or favoring by SMCL, and the Library's use of this site/service shall not be used for advertising or product endorsement purposes.

11. Contact Person: You may contact [Library name] via [insert preferred method, whether through the message option of the site/service or other option, listing a name or position title as appropriate]. In addition, [Library name] may be contacted by telephone at [add main Library number].

    (a) *In addition, if the Library plans to collect contact information by way of the site/service allowing users to opt-in to announcements, it must draft a section titled "Dissemination of Information," as follows. If the Library needs assistance, it should contact County Counsel for help drafting this section. The section should read as follows:*

12. Dissemination of Information: [Library name] will allow users/subscribers to opt-in to receiving information or notifications in relation to the Library's use of this site. The Library will only use the list for dissemination of the following kinds of information for the following purposes: [insert description of information to be disseminated and purposes of distribution]. Users/subscribers that are interested in receiving information or announcements on a periodic basis must opt-in to receiving such information, and subscribers are permitted to remove themselves from the announcement list at any time by contacting the listed representative of the Library. The Library will not release the list of subscribers except as authorized by law, and the Library will not use the list except as outlined in the Library's posted policy regarding use of the list.

(e) Information Only Forum
    1. Terms of Use
    2. Purpose: The [Library name] has decided to use this site/service for the purpose of [insert detailed description of purpose(s), being as specific as possible]. The [Library name]'s use of this site/service is being done as deemed advisable by that Library, which may decide to change or eliminate its use of this site/service.
    3. Limitations on Use: It is the intent of [Library name] only to share information through its use of this site/service for the purpose(s) listed above. The use of this site/service does not permit comments to be posted directly by other users of this site/service but instead is intended for dissemination of information to interested users or subscribers. To the extent other users wish to share information or have questions, concerns, or comments about the content of this site/service, they may contact the Library via [insert method]. [Library name] reserves the right to re-post questions, comments, or other information provided by users to [Library name], for example by the creation of a frequently asked questions (FAQ) list or any other method, but such use of information submitted

is done at the sole discretion of [Library name] and constitutes the sharing of relevant information by [Library name] rather than by any individual who submits information.

4. Statement Regarding Terms of Use and Privacy: Use of this site/service is subject to the terms of use of the site/service, including the privacy policies of the site/service, which can be found here: [insert link to the website's terms of use (for example, www.facebook.com/terms.php)]. Anyone posting comments or submitting information to [Library Name] on this site/service should keep this in mind. In addition, the poster of comments or information to this site/service agrees that his or her comments may be treated by SMCL as a public record subject to disclosure pursuant to Cal. Gov't Code Section 6250 et seq., regardless of whether such comments actually constitute a public record. Posters are urged to protect their privacy and should consider refraining from posting personally identifying information, including but not limited to: last name, address, age, and phone number. To the extent this site/service is open to the public, the public has access to its content and can access that content without the assistance of the Library or SMCL.

5. Responsibility for Content: Except for information disseminated by the owner/manager of this [blog, fan page, etc.], any information posted or submitted by others expresses the views of the person submitting such information and not necessarily the views of SMCL or the Library, and neither SMCL nor the Library is responsible for the opinions and information shared by others.

6. Disclaimer of Notice: Communications made through this site/service shall in no way be deemed to constitute legal notice to SMCL or any of its agencies, officers, employees, agents, or representatives

with respect to any existing or potential claim or cause of action against SMCL or any of its agencies, officers, employees, agents, or representatives where notice to SMCL is required by any federal, state or local law, rule or regulation.

7. Advertising: Users of this site/service should understand that contextual advertising as appears on this site/service is byproduct of use of the site/service. [Library name] does not control the site or service's placement or use of such advertising, and in no way does the use by [Library name] of this site or service constitute any endorsement or support of any such advertisements. Reference in such advertisements or in any user-generated content herein to any specific commercial products, process, or service by trade name, trademark, manufacturer, or otherwise does not constitute or imply endorsement, recommendation, or favoring by SMCL, and the Library's use of this site/service shall not be used for advertising or product endorsement purposes.

8. Contact Person: You may contact [Library name] via [insert preferred method, whether through the message option of the site/service or other option, listing a name or position title as appropriate]. In addition, [Library name] may be contacted by telephone at [add main Library number].

   (a) *In addition, if the Library plans to collect contact information by way of the site/service allowing users to opt-in to announcements, it must draft a section titled "Dissemination of Information," as follows. If the Library needs assistance, it should contact County Counsel for help drafting this section. The section should read as follows:*

9. Dissemination of Information: [Library name] will allow users/subscribers to opt-in to receiving information or notifications in relation to the Library's use

of this site. The Library will only use the list for dissemination of the following kinds of information for the following purposes: [insert description of information to be disseminated and purposes of distribution]. Users/subscribers that are interested in receiving information or announcements on a periodic basis must opt-in to receiving such information, and subscribers are permitted to remove themselves from the announcement list at any time by contacting the listed representative of the Library. The Library will not release the list of subscribers except as authorized by law, and the Library will not use the list except as outlined in the Library's posted policy regarding use of the list.

(7) SOCIAL MEDIA WORK PLAN TEMPLATE

Need help? Contact the Communications Manager in the Director's Office.

Section I: Library Information

For all social media channels, Libraries are required to submit a Social Media Work Plan to the Communications Manager to review, make recommendations and keep on record. Draft Social Media Work Plans may go through more than one cycle of the revision and review process before such work plans are ready for approval by the Library Manager or designee and the Director's Office. It's recommended that each Library keep a copy of their own Social Media Work Plan on file.

1. Library & Division:			
2. Your Name:		3. E-mail:	
4. Library Social Media Manager/PIO:		5. Social Media Manager(s):	
6. Today's Date:		7. Launch Date:	
8. Provide a brief overview of your project.			
9. Which social media channels (e.g., Facebook, Twitter) are you planning to use, and why?			

Section II: Strategy

Libraries should consider SMCL branding, goals, target audiences and success metrics for social media. The Social Media Work Plan is designed to be a conversation starter.

GOALS	**1. What are the big-picture reasons for doing this?** *(e.g., raise awareness for a new program)*
OBJECTIVES	**2. What specific actions will help you reach your goals?** *(e.g., share 3–4 Facebook posts per week)*
AUDIENCE	**3. Who is the target audience? Explain why these social media channels are a good fit.**
METRICS	**4. What does success look like? How will you know you have achieved your goals? What's your exit strategy if the site fails desired results and you need to deactivate the site?**

Section III: Process & Management

San Mateo County Libraries should choose the right social media channels that complement existing communications channels and reach key audiences.

PROMOTION	**1. How will you promote and integrate social media into your existing communications plan?**
PUBLISHING	**2. Who is authorized to use these social media channels? How much time should they spend on it?**
VISION	**3. How will your social media channels comply with our Shared Vision 2025?**
INFLUENCERS	**4. Who are some partner organizations or stakeholders that you can interact with online?**

RECORDS	**5. Follow these steps to ensure your channel is meeting records retention guidelines.**
	• Do not assume third-party platforms such as Facebook and Twitter will keep accurate records of your content—they are under no obligation to do so. • All content should be fully accessible to any person requesting documents from that site. • No records should be deleted without cause. Such removal must be done in compliance with the Social Media Policy, Terms of Use & upon consultation with Counsel. • For help archiving, consult with Technology and Counsel.
TERMS OF USE	**6. Determine which kind of First Amendment forum you wish to create for Terms of Use (See Legal Concerns in Social Media Policy) and identify any legal issues that may come into play, if at all.**

Section IV: Appendix

Social media use increased 37% across all age groups in 2012, but half of Internet users 65-and-older still don't use social media. 73% of online adults use a social networking site (2013 Pew Research Report on Social Media). Statistics below published by Business Intelligence (Sept. 2013).

Trends and demographics (U.S. only):

- **Facebook** accounts for 66% of all social media sharing on mobile devices. Audience skews young, but the 45–54 age range has grown 45% since 2012.
- **Twitter** users tend to be from urban and suburban areas, with an eye toward news and information. Also, 25% of Hispanics and African-Americans on Twitter compared with 14% of whites.
- **Instagram** has the largest audience of women (68%) and people under 35 (90%).
- **LinkedIn** has the white-collar audience and skews toward men (61%). It also offers the least diversity, with 80% of its users identifying as white.
- **Pinterest** is dominated by tablet users, and 84% of users are women.
- **Google+** is the most male-oriented social network (70%), and 50% of users are between 18–24.
- **Nextdoor** serves more than 30,000 neighborhoods across 50 states, partnering with 90 government agencies since its launch in 2011.

Social media channels approved by SMCL:

- Facebook
- Twitter
- YouTube
- Flickr

- Pinterest
- Instagram
- LinkedIn
- Google+
- Blogs (e.g., WordPress)

- Vimeo
- Nextdoor
- Tumblr

Social media channels and what they're good for:

Name	Easy to manage	Good for media	Good for employees	Good for web traffic	Good for community	Good for video	Good for images
Facebook	•		•		•	•	•
Twitter	•	•		•	•		
YouTube		•	•			•	
Flickr	•	•	•				•
Pinterest	•		•	•	•		•
Instagram	•				•		•
LinkedIn	•		•		•		
Google+	•		•	•	•	•	•
Blogs		•	•	•	•	•	•
Vimeo		•	•			•	
Nextdoor	•		•	•	•		
Tumblr		•	•		•	•	•

Questions or comments:

Please contact the Communications Manager.

Rev. Sept., 2015. Sources: San Mateo County Library Social Media Policy, San Mateo County Social Media Policy (4/15), California School Boards Association

Index

About the Authors

Valerie Forrestal is the web services librarian and an assistant professor at the College of Staten Island, City University of New York. She holds an MA in media production from Emerson College, an MLIS from Rutgers University, and an MS in service-oriented computing from Stevens Institute of Technology. Valerie has written and spoken extensively about web development, social media, technology planning, and innovation in libraries and higher ed. You can find her online at vforrestal.com and vforrestal.info or on Twitter @vforrestal. You can also find her @vforrestal on Instagram if you enjoy looking at pictures of cats.

Tinamarie Vella is the library manager at the Craig Newmark Graduate School of Journalism at the City University of New York (CUNY). Vella earned an MLIS from Long Island University and an MA in English from Brooklyn College. She was named an American Library Association Emerging Leader in 2011 and has held numerous leadership positions within the organization. Her academic focus is on research trends, diversity and leadership, and media and cultural studies. Tinamarie tweets personally @tinamarievella and institutionally @newmarkresearch.